WHAT IN THE WORLD!

WILD, WEIRD, AND WONDERFUL ADVENTURES OF A WANDERER

By Michael Smith

East West Discovery Press

Published by:
East West Discovery Press
P.O. Box 2393, Gardena, CA 90247
Phone: 310-532-1115, Fax: 310-768-8926
Website: www.eastwestdiscovery.com

Editor: Gillian Dale
Copy Editor: Marcie Rouman
Book design and production: Albert Lin

Library of Congress Cataloging-in-Publication Data
Smith, Michael, 1961-
  What in the world! : wild, weird, and wonderful adventures of a wanderer / by Michael Smith.
    p. cm.
  ISBN-13: 978-0-9669437-4-0 (alk. paper)
  ISBN-10: 0-9669437-4-0 (alk. paper)
  1. Smith, Michael, 1961---Travel. 2. Voyages and travels. I. Title.
  G465.S626 2007
  910.4--dc22
                              2006009371

ISBN-10: 0-9669437-4-0
ISBN-13: 978-0-9669437-4-0

First edition 2007
Printed in China
Published in the United States of America

Acknowledgments:

I am profoundly grateful to the people described
in the following pages. Though some of them may
not see the experiences I relate as entertaining, I
do not mean any disrespect. Cultures are different,
and those differences make our world a very
interesting place.

TABLE OF CONTENTS

PREFACE

At nineteen, the last thing on my mind was travel. Taking a full load at college in the morning and working full time in the evening did not allow me many choices. Sleeping in that old Volvo station wagon and showering at the school gym was not a luxurious lifestyle either, but I was able not only to support myself through school but even to save a little money. Still, traveling abroad was certainly not in my plans with such limited time or funds.

But then something happened. Walking through a bookstore one day, I noticed a title on hitchhiking in Europe. Finishing up a stressful semester, I managed to get a leave of absence from work as well, and, only a few days after first getting the idea, my life had changed forever. Now, twenty-five years after that first fateful trip, my passion remains. Every year or so, I get a few dollars together and take off for as long as possible, exploring a different part of the planet each time. With only a small backpack, and on a small budget, going the way the wind blows me has led me to one adventure after another.

I'm a family man now, and the adventures have changed a bit. But our daughters can carry their own packs, and upon returning from our trip to Japan, one asked me that most serious question any travel-lover faces: "Why do we have to go back home?" The bug has clearly bitten them, too.

The vignettes in this book represent only fragments of some thirty trips and are presented roughly in reverse chronological order, though I tried to keep episodes in the same regions together. I hope you will enjoy vicariously experiencing some of what the world has offered me.

World Map

1 Syria
2 Egypt
3 China
4 Bhutan
5 Malaysia
6 Vietnam
7 Laos
8 Cambodia

9 Thailand
10 The Philippines
11 Indonesia
12 Bangladesh
13 India
14 Myanmar
15 Japan
16 Ghana

U.S.A. 30
Mexico 21
Ecuador 20
Denmark 22
Germany 29
Switzerland 28
Norway 27
Benin 18
Ghana 16
Togo 17

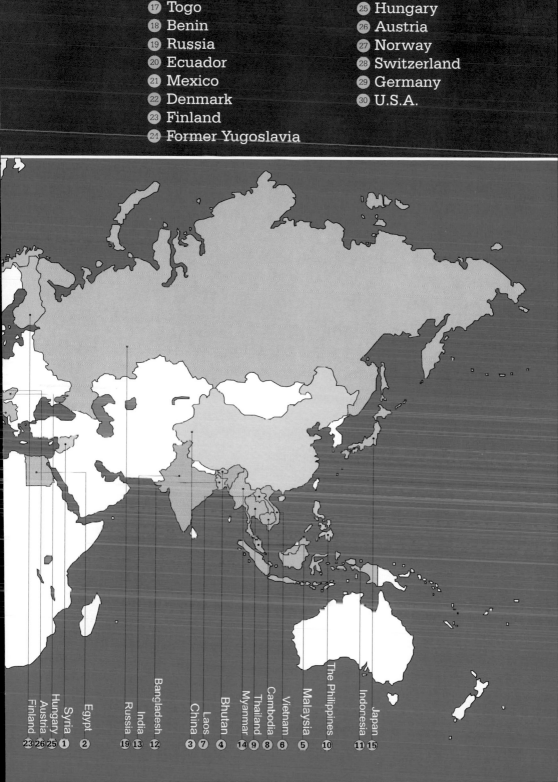

TRAVEL NECESSITIES

The following accessories are usually what I bring in a small backpack:

- Books
- Special quick-dry clothes (so they can be washed every night)
- Camera
- Jacket
- Toothbrush
- Hand wipes
- Shaver
- Tissue
- Water-purifying pills
- Lighter
- Sunscreen
- Absorbent towel
- Soap
- Whistle
- Batteries
- String
- Hand sanitizer
- Knife
- Flashlight
- Headlamp
- Bug repellent
- Bandages
- Safety pins
- Fire starter
- Tape
- Space blanket
- Candle
- Sewing kit
- Padlock
- Thermometer
- Compass
- Ear plugs
- Salt
- Water filter
- Some food and water
- Pen, pad, and more recently a PDA to write in

Backpack contents ⌃

"I offer no apologies for any departures from the usual style of travel-writing that may be charged against me—for I think I have seen with impartial eyes, and I am sure I have written at least honestly, whether wisely or not."

—*Innocents Abroad*, Mark Twain

SYRIA

My new friend and I, Palmyra, Syria

Palmyra is the remains of an ancient Roman city, isolated far in the desert between Syria's capital, Damascus, and the Iraqi border. Walking among the skeletal buildings and imposing columns, I tried to imagine how life was two thousand years ago, but my reverie was interrupted by a dog barking, growling, and staring at me from behind a pillar. I stopped moving toward him, stood still, and did not look directly at him. Still, the barking got more intense, and as he approached me, I started to back away. For every foot I retreated, though, he came closer by two or three.

When he got close enough, I could see he was not healthy. In fact, if any dog ever had the mange, it was this one. He was missing some fur and had several oozing sores on his back. As he got even closer, barking harder and harder, I nervously positioned my backpack to block him. There were a lot of stones around from the fallen pillars, but most were too heavy to throw. He was getting closer. I did not want to make any sudden or obvious movements, but remembering the pepper spray deep in my pack, I tried to reach for it. But it was too far down near the bottom, and it was too late. I was willing to panic, but did not know whether to kick him, run, try for a rock, or stay still. He was only a few feet away when, in desperation, I thought I'd throw him a piece of turkey jerky from my pocket.

He immediately quieted down. After throwing him another piece, I walked toward him, and he backed away. As I continued on my way, he began to follow at a comfortable distance, wagging his tail. We shared a few more pieces of jerky and ended up spending several hours together, wandering around the ruins like old friends.

Ancient arena, Palmyra

Building skeleton, Palmyra

∧ Decaying road-front architecture, Palmyra

Fort perched on mountain protecting, Palmyra ⌄

Sunset in Palmyra ❯

Bedouin goatherds in central Syria living as they did for a thousand years—except for maybe the guy who said he could not be disturbed because he was online.

Gentlemen relaxing at their tent
in the Syrian desert

In some countries where Islam is the dominant religion, men virtually never speak socially to a woman unless she is a close relative. Comparatively, Syria is not terribly conservative in this regard, but it is still not the West.

One well-educated couple was curious about where I was from and invited me for a snack; like most Syrians, they were extremely hospitable to a stranger. We chatted for a while about the Middle East and related issues. The conversation was curious, though, in that he would always answer for her. And, even though she could speak English perfectly well, she would ask her questions through him. When I asked if I could take a picture of them, before she had a chance to speak, her husband jumped in and said, "Sure, she would love that."

A Syrian Bedouin wearing his traditional farwa, an overcoat made from twenty lambskins

Dates for sale, a tasty Syrian snack ⌃

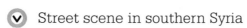

Street scene in southern Syria

A ride on this donkey cart helped me keep to my budget.

Strolling through a Damascus outdoor market, I watched a man with four well-dressed but veiled wives. They passed several jewelry shops and a butcher's market. They seemed to want to rest and stood next to the only place around to sit: a dusty, three-foot-high wall. While the women waited, the husband ran around and finally found four pieces of paper and cardboard. One at a time, he put the pieces on the top of the wall; and one at a time, each woman sat down on her piece. He then ran to get them all something to eat. The first wife got ice cream, but then each one seemed to want something different. Reflecting on all this, I concluded that multiple wives would only mean a lot of work!

Lively Damascus street scene ⌃

Many men in Syria have multiple wives. Some guys have their mother around to help out too.

Butcher with camel head for sale

Umayyad Mosque in Syria's capital, Damascus

In a Damascus cafe, I met a lady who was especially attractive. We talked, and she gave me some good advice on what to see in the city. I was really impressed with her friendliness, and before saying goodbye, I told her I thought she was amazingly open for a Syrian Muslim female. In response, she told me, "I'm a Christian from Lebanon."

‹ Nice-looking door

⌄ Distinguished gentlemen

Donkeys are still a common form of transportation in rural Syria.

Syria's Roman antiquities are amongst the best preserved in the world.

In southern Syria, not far from the Jordanian and Israeli borders, I came across an archaeology dig. Many locations in the region have been continuously inhabited for hundreds of years, and some even for thousands. These particular ruins were in a village where some ancient walls were being excavated. A boy came up and offered me a bag of about twenty coins. The coins looked authentic, but what do I know about old coins? He said that he had found them near where the university people had been digging and was trying to find someone to sell them to. He said that foreigners did not come there very often, that the bag of coins was worth about $10, and that he would sell them to me for the same.

In my mind, one of two things was certain: Either this was an incredible opportunity, or, more likely, he was offering me a bag of worthless junk—imitations perfectly designed for a greedy tourist to get what they deserved. But there were no tourists anywhere around here, and my experience with Syrians so far had been overwhelmingly positive. Despite its reputation abroad, I had received only continual kindness and hospitality from everyone I had met here. Holding the coins, what was in my mind were visions of being praised or handsomely rewarded as I donated them to a museum or something. So, I gave him about $10 and took my chances.

Back home, I made an appointment with a numismatic expert—one who would give me a real surprise. Without knowing how much I had paid for them or how I had obtained them, he correctly identified the part of the world where they'd come from and other details about the coins, and concluded by saying they were, in fact, authentic. "Wow," I thought to myself, feeling quite excited. He then added that though very old, these coins were actually quite common; many of them had been produced. All together, he said, they were worth about $10.

Fruit stand

Gentlemen enjoying conversation

Excavation of ancient town in southern Syria

EGYPT

Taxis are the best way to get around in most Egyptian towns. Just put your hand out, shake it a bit and a few seconds later you're on your way. But negotiating the price, so important for most other transactions in Egypt, is different with taxis. The meter is not used, and if you politely ask the driver how much it will cost to a destination, he may quote ten times the going rate. If, however, you get in, state your destination, and get out when you arrive, you can pass through the window what amounts to be a very small sum, maybe equal to one or two dollars. But how can you know exactly how much to pay? I asked a local. "Just ask anyone," he said, "except the driver."

ⓥ Homes in Alexandria

< Building, Cairo

One of the remaining wonders of the world, the great pyramids

Donkey with heavy load

 Nightlife in vibrant Cairo

 Hieroglyphics at Edfu

Goats, sheep, and a cow awaiting their date with destiny, pre-Eid animal sacrificing, Alexandria

After some nice people invited me to drink tea and walk through the ruins, I found a men's room and stood in front of a urinal doing what one might expect, when the attendant handed me a three-foot piece of toilet paper. I was perplexed by this. Once before in a public restroom, an attendant handed me and another man standing there tissue, right while we were relieving ourselves. Very strange indeed. This time, something occurred to me, an adage as old as the Pharaohs: "No matter how you jump and dance, the last few drops go down your pants."

< The Luxor temple

v Ave. of the Sphinx at Luxor temple

When in Rome be a Roman, self portrait

Granite obelisk, Luxor temple

Ancient gods beautifully carved in stone, Luxor temple

The tomb of King Tutankhamen, Valley of the Kings

Ramesseum, Thebes

❮ Workers in the Valley of the Kings

❮ Silhouettes of a shepherd and kids

❮ Riding in comfort

❮ I told him that oasis was just a mirage.

Elephantine Island was once a bustling business center for trading pachyderm products. But the busy life has gone with the extinction of Egyptian elephants. Though Nubians have a long and fascinating history, today the sleepy villagers seem to take life pretty easy.

Nubian villages of Siou and Kotu on Elephantine Island in the upper Nile, with a labyrinth of pathways and homes having interesting doors, not two of which seem to be alike.

CHINA

The Great Wall of China

Rice, more than just food in China, its production offers artistic patterns of beauty.

From Guiping, my intention was to find the Dragon Pool Forest, a national park protecting a last remaining section of old-growth forest in Guangxi province. Along the way, somehow I was misdirected and managed to get on a boat going somewhere else. This boat was a noisy bucket of rusty steel and rotting wood, with about fifty passengers aboard. It would stop from time to time at the bottom edge of the steep cliffs that formed the gorge, dropping off or picking up passengers near villages that were apparently hiding beyond the cliffs. The villages got fewer and farther between, and it became clear I had made a navigational error.

I looked for help from some fellow passengers, and many got involved in the conversation; in fact, everyone on the boat was looking at me, but the only thing I understood for certain was that I had no idea what they were talking about. They were not speaking Mandarin or Cantonese but a dialect called Bit Tan, of which I knew not one word.

Approximating our location on the map with the help of a compass, I was not aided by the many talking away at me at once. Finally, one man, whose speech I was able to understand, conveyed that we were going to a region by the same name, Bit Tan. When we finally arrived at the last village of the run, the man said that the only way in or out was by that boat and that the boat would now be shut down for the day. It was a picturesque setting, but I was getting hungry and there were no familiar noodle shops to eat at or any other eating place, for that matter; worse still, it was late in the day by now, and there were no accommodations.

Cliff with hidden village near Wuxuan

 My new friends on a boat going up river from Guiping

A common food in southern China is snake. Here my dinner is getting away.

The man who had gotten off with me understood my predicament and gestured to me to come with him. I had little choice, and of course I was ecstatic, realizing the alternative was to sleep on the ground, muddy and wet from a recent rain. We walked up and around several hills. He stopped to introduce me to his grandparents at their modest mud house, then we went on a ways more until we got to his even more secluded home up high on a hill. He was seventeen years old and lived with his two younger brothers while their parents were away for months at a time, working in a city. The home had a large garden in front and the backdrop was of spectacular mountain peaks.

Beautiful river near Bit Ton

Terraced rice paddy

When it was time for dinner, the two younger boys, about ten and fifteen, went to the field and picked some vegetables. Grandpa brought some fish and started a wood fire under the stove in the cooking hut outside the house. When the wok was hot, they stir-fried everything and we ate a delicious dinner.

As the sky darkened, the rain began, and the thunder and lightning off in the distance silhouetted the mountains. It was a very pleasant place to be and the polite hostess's hospitality was exceptional. I particularly appreciated their kindness not just for the obvious reasons, but especially because they were rural farmers, quite poor. There was no running water in a kitchen, no phone, no clock or heater. No desperately needed air conditioner, no refrigerator or other common conveniences. There was electric power, but it was intermittent and the lights would dim from time to time. There was one other thing, though, that showed they were in the modern age: a TV with DVD player. After dinner, it was time to turn the volume loud and watch an American movie. It was Sylvester Stallone starring in *Rambo*.

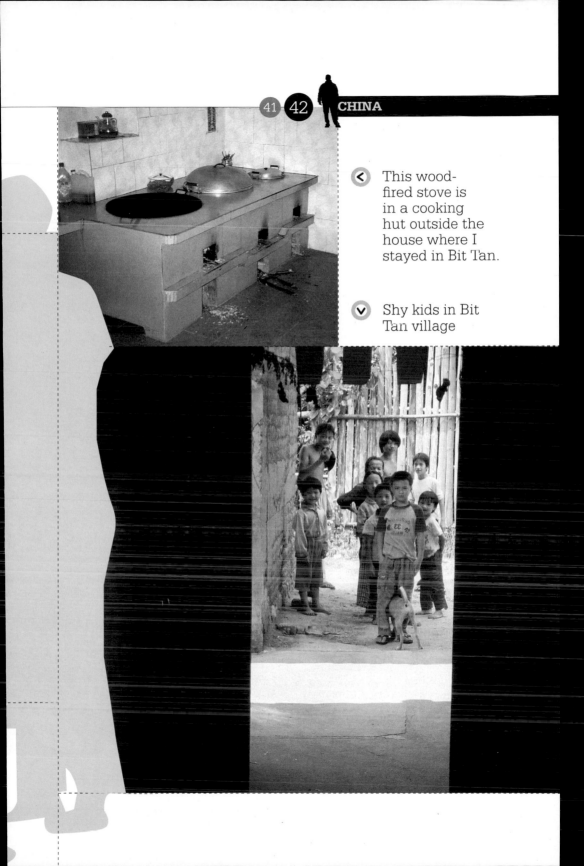

This wood-fired stove is in a cooking hut outside the house where I stayed in Bit Tan.

Shy kids in Bit Tan village

Kowloon Estates in Kowloon, Hong Kong

The concrete jungle of Hong Kong has the reputation of a capitalist "paradise" and it is, with its skyscrapers and business-friendly atmosphere. But for most of its years, poverty has also been endemic. Boat people managed a meager existence and many all over the former colony lived in squalor. One of the places with an especially bad reputation was called Kowloon Estates. Somewhat of an outlaw area, it lacked effective control from either mainland China or the Hong Kong authorities. I was with a local friend who said this place was dangerous; she had never been inside, but if I wanted to see it, maybe we would be safe exploring together. After all, my being a *gwai lo* (foreign devil) might intimidate the bad guys.

Kowloon Estates was a massive complex with structures ranging from nine- to fifteen-stories high; a labyrinth as wide as a large city block. Walking the pathways, it was easy to get lost, as it was obviously "designed" by simply adding one section to the next. Being a place where gangsters hung out and the police would usually stay away, there were all kinds of illegal activities. Exposed pipes and barrels dripped with strange chemicals, and illicit shops abounded. The first place we passed was a dentist's office—though it looked more like a car repair shop. A man lay back in an especially ugly dental chair to get a tooth fixed. The cost in a place like this is never more than a few dollars, but it looked quite unsanitary. There was also a hospital where surgery was performed on the cheap.

There were rats and cockroaches, and we passed some mean-looking men who told us not to come back that direction. We came to what looked like a dead end, but it was so dark it was hard to tell. Up a stairwell in nearly pitch darkness, two eyes were looking back. They seemed too small to be human until, adjusting to the low light, we saw the silhouette of a little boy, naked, maybe three years old, standing still in the rubbish. He was spooky though, rather than cute. We followed many passageways like the scariest of movie sets, trying to find a way out. There were strange storefronts with bad smells emanating from them and who-knows-what for sale. We finally found our way to the other end of the walled city and escaped, feeling that seeing this place once was more than enough.

⌃ A skinny cat and dog in danger of being eaten by one of the huge local rats

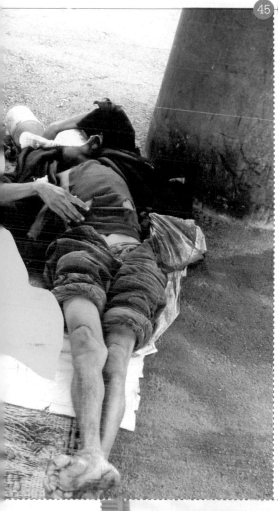

Homeless man in Hong Kong

China's sudden explosive economic growth is exemplified near Hong Kong here in Shen Zhen. When I visited this spot in 1984, it was a simple fishing village being readied for an experiment in capitalism. It worked.

Negotiating the price of a room is a "must" to get a good deal in many places, but especially in China. After a few dirty $10 rooms, I wanted some luxury. A travel book said this four-star beach resort hotel might have a room rate equivalent to more than $100 but to ask for discounts. That turned out to be good advice. Walking into the palatial lobby, I was given the rate sheet at reception that said, "Special—$90." I then asked for a discount and was told a new figure of about $50, without an ocean view. I said the lack of ocean view did not matter but it still cost too much. She said I should see the room. I did, and it was outstanding, with not only an ocean view but also a sandy beach just outside the glass door. Perfection.

I walked back to reception ready to take the room. I said that it did, in fact, have a view but asked if that was the best price she could offer. She asked me where I was from and where I was going and what I was doing so far away from home. Knowing that foreigners often pay a higher price than locals, I was wary. But this was a remote tropical resort area on Hainan Island near Vietnam and far away from the frantic big-city attitude. In her soft voice, she said that she was very pleased I had come so far and that the room, if I wanted it, all included, would be the equivalent of $24.

< Fancy hotel on Hainan Island

L Comfortable beach life of Hainan Island

v Hiking trail to a monkey sanctuary in southern China

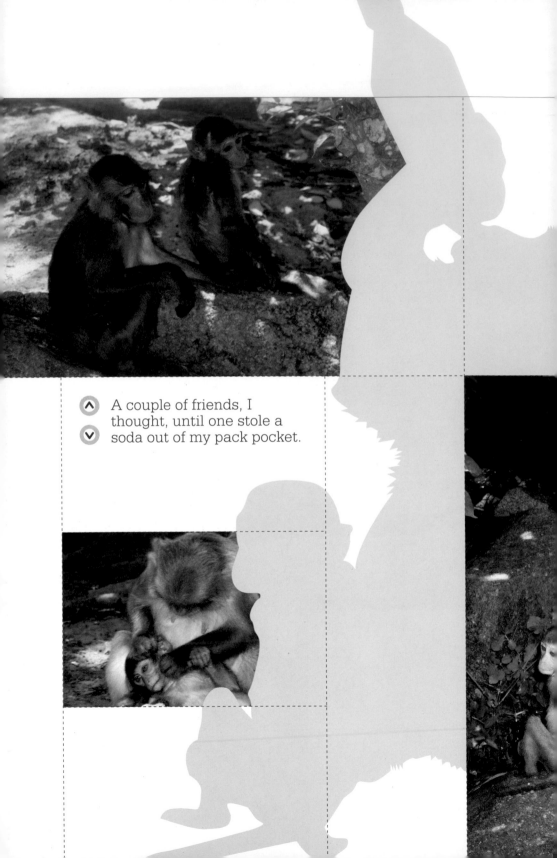

A couple of friends, I thought, until one stole a soda out of my pack pocket.

> A nice lady wanted to practice English, but she said I had to pay her a dollar to do so.

< In an instant, he bit through the bottom of the bottle and drank the whole thing.

Restaurant menus in rural China are rarely available in English, especially those offering local specialties. One place in Yunnan did offer an interesting English menu, albeit oddly spelled.

English Menu

rabit with chilly oil
mixed kelp
stripfried kidneys
edible fungus
stewed pigs liveir
couple lung pieces
wild prickle made with chicken paws
mustard tuber
rabit with wild prickley
bitter vegitable
naxi blood in pork intestine
oil yak meat
fried eggs fish
cow liveir
starch
mudsnail with leek sprouts
fried dragonflies
carp with pigs liveir
fried tree skin
pepper fish
Canadian whisky

A comfortable restaurant table in Lijiang

Waitress

My delicious
pepper fish

Friendly Naxi girl

Babbling brook of Lijiang old town ⌄

A classic town street, Lijiang

Elders conversing

A friendly elderly woman

Pathway carved into the solid
rock of Tiger Leaping Gorge

Gaining some elevation into
the alpine zone

Pathway into the clouds of Yulong Xueshan in Yunnan Province

I enjoyed climbing to 4,600 meters at the glacier near Mt. Satseto in the foothills of the Tibetan plateau.

From outside my window, the yelp of a dog broke into my slumber. I was trying to sleep in after a long trip to this village near the Burmese border. But it was about 9 a.m. and the noises from the market and the dogs below woke me. I went downstairs, had a delicious soup—noodle with some interesting-tasting meat—and then walked around the market. Farmwomen were hawking an excellent selection of fresh vegetables, and butchers hacked away at meat hanging from hooks in the open air. Ducks, rabbits, pigs, chickens, and fish looked back at me, most still alive but soon to be slaughtered. They were killed by a break of the neck or a slit of the throat, then cut up into pieces and quickly sold to the next customer.

Walking through one passage, I came upon a cage full of about twenty dogs, all cute and all jammed in together. Then a man took a large pair of tongs and grabbed one by the neck and with his other hand clubbed the dog in the head as it yelped, just for a few seconds. Now I knew where the sound I had heard all morning came from. Its body would be cut in pieces and, as fast as the man would slice, a customer would come by and purchase a piece of meat. I walked further, past some cats and kittens meowing, also crammed as tight as could be into small cages. Someone's lunch. I walked out of the market feeling queasy, wondering just what kind of meat I had had in my soup only a few minutes before.

Fish for sale, swimming in an inch of water ❯

In a village near the Burmese border, I wandered through a marketplace where fresh sauces, spices, vegetables, and other delicacies were attractively displayed.

Enjoying the standard breakfast – a bowl of noodle soup

Live ducks bound together

 Dogs and cats before and after slaughter

Man with extra hats
in Guangxi province

⌃ Southern Chinese folks on a scooter

⌃ On the way to toil in the rice field

⌄ Rice field

The green scenery of
southeast China

A man on a traditional
bamboo raft catches up
with a ferry to peddle
his goods.

木事停车场

FOREIGNERBUSPARKINGPOT

A buffalo is pulled by his nostrils with a string.

Parking pot?

The famous mountains near Yangshuo in southern China

BHUTAN

In peaceful Bhutan, barking dogs are the main source of noise pollution. They are not encouraged to quiet down, because of a belief that they scare off evil spirits. Though often running around in packs snapping at one another, they are not aggressive toward people. An old man told me that all the dogs in Bhutan eat rice and behave well.

On a hike in the foothills of the Himalayas, one particular dog befriended me. He appeared out of nowhere and would stop and go when I did. We kept up a pretty good pace, and though I am in good shape, it was a steep hill and we were huffing and puffing, his tongue hanging out. We thought we were going fast—until three old women in their seventies or eighties going in the same direction flew by us. The sharp rocks on the trail were difficult for us to maneuver, but not hard for these grannies, who were all barefoot. Even with big packs on their backs and more bags in their arms, they passed us like we were standing still. The dog and I just looked at each other.

Here I began my trek to the Taktsang Goemba (Tiger's Nest), Bhutan's most famous monastery.

Deep in the forest, this odd-looking obstacle got in the way, but as I glanced away and back, he was gone.

> Taktsang Goemba Monastery precariously perched on the mountainside.

∨ Stream coming from the Himalayas

Definitely man's best friend, this guy came out of nowhere to guide me to the monastory seen in the background; the site attracting many pilgrims clings precariously to the rock face a thousand feet above the canyon floor.

Large homes are the norm in Bhutan, but roads are few and far between. Getting home can be a very long walk. Footpaths traverse the landscape with breathtaking scenery, making the walk worthwhile.

Pathways to
homes; few
buildings in
Bhutan have
uninteresting
architecture.

National Library

Festival in the capital city, Timphu

Dancing priests use phallic symbols to bless young women and enhance their fertility.

Citizens of Bhutan are required by law to wear the national costume.

A boy monk peers through the window after morning prayers.

Monk children at prayer

∧ School room

∨ Millions of marijuana plants grow wild in Bhutan.

MALAYSIA

Cooking our food in Kelantan province

Muslim girls

In an outdoor eating place in a small town in northern
Malaysia, some girls, all wearing Muslim headscarves,
invited me to their table. One explained that she did not
like to see a foreigner sitting alone. They were fun to talk
with, and the fish they shared with me was excellent. After
a while, one girl removed her scarf. When I inquired why,
she explained she often does this when she knows her
grandmother has gone to sleep. She was careful to add that
she was a good Muslim, except for an occasional beer with
her girlfriends.

Railway station in central
Peninsular Malaysia

Tissue dispenser in a guest house—but a bit too far away!

Child close to his mommy

‹ Measuring sticks at a river in northern Malaysia show how the water can rise twelve meters after it rains. The dock at the bottom floats up and down on the water.

› After a walk in the tropical sun, this well-deserved Kickapoo juice hit the spot.

‹ Outdoor birdcages in northern Malaysia

On a hike in the Malaysian national park of Tama Negara, the trail narrowed and the forest noises—mostly from insects—were almost deafening. A branch shook above me, and straight up through the forest's canopy I saw a large face that looked as startled as I was; it belonged to a primate of some sort, just about my size. We both froze and stared at each other for several seconds; then, almost like an explosion from branch to branch, he was gone. I kept looking up into trees to find him—until a long snake crossed the path in front of me and turned my attention back to earth.

The forest of Taman Negara

Not seeing much with my flashlight in the pitch-black cave, the photos revealed many bats.

River through Tama Negara forest

These villagers of the Tama Negara jungle were friendly. One took me to their cave.

The forest people of Peninsular Malaysia are called Orang Asli. They live mostly self sufficient, hunting the wildlife.

Orang Asli of the Tama Negara jungle

Showing off his weapons

< Blowpipe guns

< Poison darts used with a blowpipe

∨ Pet bird

VIETNAM

Portable
Vietnamese noodle
restaurant

Street scene in
Saigon

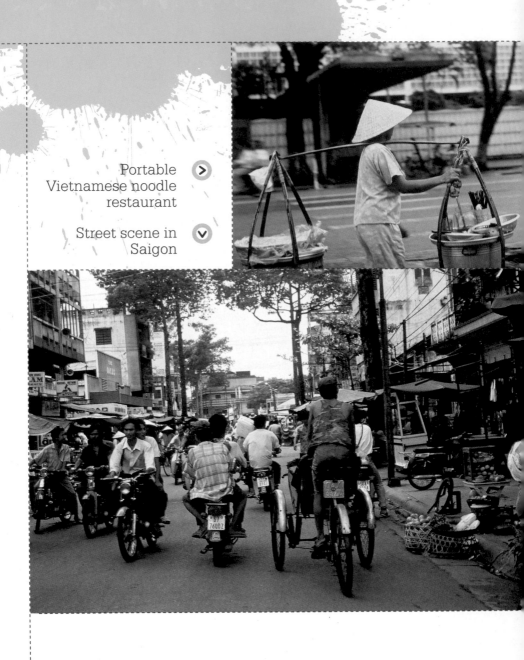

It certainly can rain in Southeast Asia! Even though I had taken a lower-class accommodation in Saigon, I thought I would be safe from the downpour on the second floor. But the torrent grew ever stronger and the whole building roared. The toilet was making strange sounds too, so I went to look. The water had drained out and it was groaning as if to tell me something. It soon quieted down; the water returned and began rising. But then the clear water turned brown and the toilet overflowed. What came out was even worse than the filth one would expect: First one, then many cockroaches and other moving things, unspeakable things, were coming out, flooding my room, and within minutes the entire floor was covered. I crouched on the bed, wondering what would happen next. The rain kept pounding so hard; the building shook, and I was even more worried about the building holding together than about the disgusting pond surrounding me.

Suddenly, the door opened and a very skinny guy with large rubber boots walked in. He looked like the janitor doing his daily rounds and he announced that he would clean up. After he worked for a while, scooping up scampering cockroaches and filth without showing any squeamishness, he finally seemed to remember me. He stopped, slowly looked up, and asked, "Would you like a different room?"

Two girls zoom around vibrant, Hanoi.

While Hmong men and boys work in the field and hunt, women do handicrafts, gather wood, and oftentimes carry heavy loads.

Hmong women and girls prepare to sell their handicrafts in Lao Chai.

Getting your goose cleaned high in the mountains also shows how easy bird flu can be transmitted to humans.

Rice terraces of northern Vietnam, an endless patchwork of beautiful designs, in Giang Ta Chu

The Red Dzao is one of Vietnam's hill tribe groups. They can be recognized with their silver beads and coins, and red turbans, near Sapa.

A Red Dzao woman walks 20 miles to town to sell her goods near Sapa.

Halong Bay has many beautiful limestone islands, but getting on may be difficult.

LAOS

A Laotian village in the "golden triangle" ❯

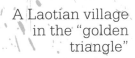

Catching small frogs for dinner ⌄

⌄ Bath time

Distilling fine rice wine ❯

It is the present-day Wild West in much of the "golden triangle," with governments having little control or influence in this area where Laos, Thailand, and Myanmar meet. I was feeling adventurous and crossed the river border from Thailand to Laos, far from any legal checkpoint. I had been told their rice wine was available and cheap, so I decided to get a better look at this part of Laos. I quickly came across some locals.

Their first offer was a large bag of marijuana, the bud of the plant, with an interesting color. I am not a weed smoker myself, but I understood this was expensive stuff. However, he said it would be only about four dollars for what I guessed to be hundreds of dollars worth of pot. When I said no, I was offered opium and shown some black gooey stuff. I knew two neighboring countries gave the death penalty to drug traffickers, so I said no to that, too. In another location, a man offered me a girl. The man said, "About $200," and pointed at a girl. I am not into prostitution, either, but I thought that that was kind of expensive for a hooker in the jungle. He called the girl, who was definitely under eighteen, and repeated his price. Then it dawned on me: He was not renting the girl but selling her; she was a human being for sale! It made me so sad; I wished I could buy her just to set her free.

This is a place run by drug lords, where police do not exist; a place where anything goes. I could be murdered with no possibility of an investigation ever taking place. But there was also a false feeling of safety with the peace on the people's faces and the greenness of the jungle village. Finally finding the moonshine rice wine I'd come for, I bought the bottle and got out of there.

CAMBODIA

> One of the many mass graves of the killing fields near Choeung Ek

Cambodia is a great country for having an adventure, with remote jungles and amazing ruins from the great Khmer civilization giving it a uniqueness all its own. But some of its modern history has been very sad. Only a few days in the country and I saw more people with missing limbs than I had in my entire life, many of them children. Millions of landmines buried in the country have been responsible, and thousands are still a threat. So, on a motor scooter to go out into the countryside, I was careful to stay on the road. The years of war were over, but making a detour onto an unmarked minefield was not a mistake I was going to make.

In Cambodia's killing fields, a monument stood to honor the hundreds of thousands murdered there, victims of the dreaded Khmer Rouge. I ended up in the place alone, with

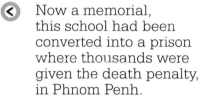

Now a memorial, this school had been converted into a prison where thousands were given the death penalty, in Phnom Penh.

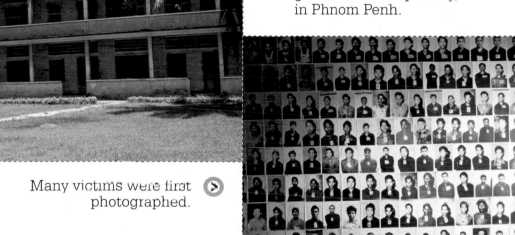

Many victims were first photographed.

time to consider the genocide. The weather was calm and warm, but approaching were big storm clouds. In the monument, the real human skulls piled up high were hard to look at. I joked to myself sarcastically that the Khmer Rouge made communism look bad. But seeing the bits of cloth from the clothes of the corpses still mixed in the dirt I was standing on, I was overwhelmed with sadness. I started to cry, something I hadn't done in maybe ten years. From the small size of many of the human skulls, I realized that again, as from the landmines, so many of the victims had been children. As I wept, it began to rain. It seemed appropriate, like tears from the heavens. I got back on the motorbike a bit traumatized and rode slowly down the road into a downpour.

Rice fields of
Cambodia

Among the most evil
men that have walked
the face of the earth,
Pol-pot and partners
were responsible for
the genocide.

A monument to those murdered by the Khmer Rouge is filled with human skulls in Choeung Ek.

Victims' skulls and clothes

THAILAND

∨ Sign to identify those with "hippy" characteristics

NOTICE

BY VIRTUE OF SECTION 16·THE IMMIGRATION ACT, B.E. 2522 (1979),
THE MINISTER OF INTERIOR ISSUES THE FOLLOWING ORDER TO IDENTIFY
AN ALIEN WITH "HIPPY" CHARACTERISTICS :

1. A PERSON WHO WEARS JUST A SINGLET OR WAISTCOAT WITHOUT UNDERWEAR.
2. A PERSON WHO WEARS SHORTS WHICH ARE NOT RESPECTABLE.
3. A PERSON WHO WEARS ANY TYPE OF SLIPPERS OR WOODEN SANDALS, EXCEPT
   WHEN THESE ARE PART OF NATIONAL COSTUME.
4. A PERSON WHO WEARS SILK PANTS THAT DO NOT LOOK RESPECTABLE.
5. A PERSON WHO HAS LONG HAIR THAT APPEARS UNTIDY AND DIRTY.
6. A PERSON WHO IS DRESSED IN AN IMPOLITE AND DIRTY-LOOKING MANNER.

AN ALIEN WITH SUCH CHARACTERISTICS WILL BE PROHIBITED FROM ENTERING
THE KINGDOM. IF AN ALIEN HAS THE ABOVE CHARACTERISTICS AFTER ENTERING
THE KINGDOM, HE WILL BE IMMEDIATELY DEPORTED.

••••••••••••••••••

AN ALIEN MUST CARRY THE MINIMUM AMOUNT OF MONEY WITH HIM WHEN
ENTERING THE KINGDOM IN ACCORDANCE WITH THE ANNOUNCEMENT OF THE MINISTRY
OF INTERIOR AS FOLLOWS :-

1. TRANSIT VISA OR WITHOUT VISA, NOT LESS THAN 5,000 BAHT PER PERSON
   OR 10,000 BAHT PER FAMILY.
2. TOURIST VISA OR NON-IMMIGRANT VISA NOT LESS THAN 10,000 BAHT PER
   PERSON OR 20,000 BAHT PER FAMILY.
3. THIS ANNOUNCEMENT DOES NOT APPLY TO CHILDREN UNDER 12 YEARS OLD.

Waterfalls in northern Thailand

I met up with a group going to spend a few days hiking in the jungle looking for some remote hill tribespeople. We were an eclectic bunch, with one or two each from Germany, Australia, Britain, Burma, and Thailand. We had a Kiren interpreter for Thai and a Thai interpreter for English. A guide of any kind is not my style, but they were very helpful, prepared the food, and only cost a few dollars a day. They were also carving out much of the trail as we walked, swinging their machetes in front. Once in the mountains, we passed a Hmong farm; these villagers were not particularly isolated with their poppy fields for opium production. After a long day's trek, deep in the jungle we found what we had come for: the mountain people. They were living as if in the Stone Age in bamboo and banana-leaf huts. The only metal I saw was a broken machete, a cooking pot, and an iron teakettle.

Through translation from English to Thai to Kerin and back, I spoke with the chief of the tribe. He was just as curious about us as we were about them. His questions were very revealing. He asked me if the trees were different where I lived. I said I only had two trees, one in front and one in back of my house. He laughed and poured more mildly intoxicating root tea into a bamboo cup. He asked how I grow rice and also about my pigs. I explained that a man sat on a tractor ("What's that?") and went for miles back and forth in a field; more disbelief. As for my pigs, I said I would get pieces from the market and put them in my icebox, but he had never heard of ice.

This isolated tribe of about forty was totally self-contained. Many hill tribespeople in the area were not as isolated as they, so our overnight stay in this most primitive village was a unique privilege.

< L Poppies grown for opium

v Water flowing from bamboo plumbing in the hill tribe village

The jungle trail

With six-inch spiders, the jungle is not a place for an arachnophobe.

High in the canopy, a four-foot-long string bean

Butterfly

I used a vine to cross the stream.

Secluded village ⌃

Yours truly getting a bit to eat: noodles wrapped in a banana leaf ❯

The Kiren hill tribespeople are found in isolated mountain forests of Southeast Asia. This group lived a day's walk from a road leading to Mai Hong Song. The young girl in front is holding dinner.

Teapot with mildly intoxicating root tea

The Thai-Laotian border is formed by the Mekong River as it winds its way from China. The room I found to stay in was an especially good deal. Besides a wonderful river view, breakfast was included, as were a porch with a hammock to relax on and a complementary foot massage. The manager also was a very nice guy wanting to practice English. The night here cost me about five dollars.

Not only were the people friendly, but the animals were, too. I had a baby monkey to play with, my cute little pal who slept in my arms while I read. The room came with a bed friend, too: a rabbit, which left me its gift on the covers. There was also a gecko on the washroom wall, inches from my nose.

< Relaxing in a hammock, I rested my feet.

< ^ Monkey friend at the Mekong River

v Shower friend (gecko)

Sunset on the
Mekong River

Comfortable room

As I was walking by a temple looking at the beautiful architecture, a monk came up to me and asked if I spoke English. He explained that their English teacher was absent, and as we walked along, he asked some more questions (apparently to see if I might qualify to help). Finally, he asked if I would teach the English class for the day. In reply, I followed him.

Thirty rowdy teenage monks (boys often become monks for a year) had just as much adolescent vigor as teenage boys would anywhere. The excitement of having a foreigner teach them was overwhelming. Some proudly spoke the English they knew, though none could finish a conversation. These were beginner monks learning beginners' English. We focused on pronunciation. After some time, I asked one of them what their hobby was. He replied, "Girls!" and the class laughed hysterically. I could not keep them in control after that. "So much for the monk lifestyle!" I thought. And someone else told me that individual female travelers in the region did not have much to worry about—except to keep their eyes open for the occasional overly-interested monk.

In Thailand, boys often become monks for a year.

Buddhism plays
a key role in Thai
culture. Temples and
statues can be found
everywhere

Huge Buddha ⌃

Monks enjoying a
magnificent waterfall ❯

⌃ This laundry business washes clothes in the river, then hangs them to dry on the bamboo.

⌄ Dogs carved from stone

In the countryside, traditional Thai massage is most often performed by blind men and older ladies and consists of two hours of being stretched, pushed, and prodded, a process that is pleasurable even if sometimes a little painful. Receiving this treatment, I quickly understood how this tradition has survived thousands of years. In Mae Hong Son, I was told to see two old ladies if my back was bothering me. I walked up the hill to an open-air kind of gazebo where they were sitting. It was dusk, and the light trickled through the leaves of a tamarind tree. After mutual greetings, I signaled to them that my lower back hurt. The one who started on me had the magic touch that gave almost immediate relief; she really knew what she was doing. I was lying down on a special table in a shelter without walls at the edge of the jungle—exquisite surroundings.

An occasional mosquito would come by, and the second lady would slap the lady massaging me. Then, as she spotted a buzzer on me, I got a whack. It happened again

The elephant, the symbol of Thailand, can be found as a labor or entertainment around the country.

and again, and she hit hard! The pleasure of the treatment and of knowing another mosquito was dead did not quite make up for the disturbing slaps. She hit so hard my whole body would jump.

After a while, another customer arrived, which I hoped would mean an end to the hitting. This patient, also an older lady, lay down next to me. As her treatment began (by the lady doing the hitting), I thought at last it would stop. Some minutes went by, and there was real peace. But the silence was broken again when I heard the other patient get a smack, and I felt her pain. Then it was my turn. A yank, cracking of my vertebrae, then another slap to make sure I enjoyed it.

Walking down the hill, I did feel better, and I was thinking that this was all an amusing experience. Then I remembered that the night mosquitoes so near the jungle often carry malaria. Suddenly, the hitting lady was OK with me after all.

Taking a swim in the jungle

◀ Down the hatch!

▶ Beautiful pond

↰ ▶

I used to eat a lot of bugs in Southeast Asia, until I found out DDT is sprayed into the jungle to catch the bugs.

THE PHILIPPINES

Some locals scampered across this bridge before me, but they were all about a third of my weight, in southern Luzon, The Philippines.

The volcano in the center of Lake Taal in Luzon Island was beautiful, even if getting there was somewhat unpleasant; in the smelly back of a fish transport truck, then across the crater lake in a small boat to the island in the middle. It was a hot day with maximum humidity, and though personally melting, I was determined to climb to the top of the attractive double-peaked island. Soon, my large bottle of water was empty, but I was not far from the top and in no time reached the summit. I had the excitement of looking from the unstable pumice gravel of the rim down into the gray, seemingly quiet crater. Then it was back down—fast—through the steam vents and sulfur smoke.

I later learned this volcano and lake were really remarkable, not just for their beauty. Nearby towns were buried under the rubble of past eruptions, and evidence of human habitation was submerged under the lake, visible only to divers. Unusual saltwater animals were living in a lake, now fresh-water, which had at one time been connected to the sea. And this volcano is just about the most deadly in the world, killing thousands over the years with forty-one eruptions since 1572; in 1911, an eruption killed 1,335 people in one big bang. And the strange ways this volcano does its deadly work include explosions of mud laced with sulfuric acid, chemically burning its victims.

At that moment, though, I was intent only on getting something to drink. And the dream came true: A man with no one around was selling sodas from an ice chest at the beach. He smiled at what may have been his biggest sale of the month and watched me gulp down all six of his cold, 7-Up-type drinks.

The Chocolate Hills of Boho

∧ >

These little creatures are the *tarsier*, the smallest primates in the world near Corella on Bohol Island.

INDONESIA

With no recent rain, the smell of Jakarta's open
sewers was an especially unpleasant reminder of
what those in a developing country must endure.
Under such circumstances, the first thing on my
mind was to find a bus out of town. Once on a long-
distance bus, the stench was gone, but the buses
on Java are driven up and down the dangerous
mountain roads at breakneck speeds. After the
poverty and pestilence of a dirty city, and the fright
from being at the edge of a cliff going at full throttle
in a bus driven by a teenager, I was happy to reach
the trailhead for another hike. Through the dense
jungle and up the mountain, I felt safe at last—
standing at the top of another active volcano.

I am not sure what it was, but I was not going to stick around and find out.

BANGLADESH

Young beggar,
one of thousands
across the
country

A city with even worse pollution than Jakarta is Dhaka, Bangladesh. The smog was horrible. If you blew your nose after spending any time on Dhaka's polluted streets, the tissue would be full of a black, chemical-looking concoction. Hundreds of beggars, many children, were all around. A six-year-old holding a naked, dirty two-year-old with hand outstretched was typical. Begging is different here than it is in the West: The blind and the many people with missing limbs as well as children get no assistance whatsoever except from street handouts. One time, I gave a sick-looking woman what would be equal to about twenty cents because I had no smaller bills. The English-speaking person nearby told me that since they only expect a few cents, the recipient would pray for me all day.

To build anything in Bangladesh, manual labor is used because the cost is negligible. Heavy equipment, even to dig out a mountainside, would be rare. Instead, hundreds of men, women, and children form a system of passing buckets. People digging ditches and breaking rocks with sledgehammers were normal scenes across the country. Some construction sites with their hard labor seemed surreal, like ant farms or medieval prison camps.

It is also one of the most challenging places to get around. Buses are barely held together, and "baby taxis"—best described as chainsaws on three wheels—zoom around spewing out lead and smoke at eardrum-breaking decibels. They are dangerous to be near, let alone ride in, but traveling in this country requires using them daily. What I can only describe as "unintended physical contact between vehicles" happened for me at least four times, both in taxis and on a minibus, when the driver smashed into an old man on a bike, then yelled something out the window and drove off. He apparently thought it was the old man's fault. All vehicles have dents and no one will stop for a mere fender bender.

Goods are piled up on the back of a tricycle.

Bangladeshis on the street

Few cars in Bangladesh are without minor scrapes and dents.

When female skin is shown, beautiful Henna hand art is sometimes revealed.

The service in Bangladesh is very good. At any hotel, even one costing $4 a night, young male bellboys will bend over backwards to offer their assistance. However, sometimes it is awkward. After carrying my small pack halfway around the world, I felt strange when they apparently thought I could not manage to carry it a few more steps to the room. Several times, they pulled it off me even when I had clearly rejected their offers of help. Other times, their help was slightly more welcome, like when I was trying to figure out how to use the plumbing. In one place, the shower had six knobs to turn and none gave me hot water. The problem was determined to be an electrical one—or so they thought.

These bellboys love to knock on the door and ask guests if they need something. Though at almost every hotel I stayed in they would come to the door more than once, even late at night, it seemed more curious than a nuisance. One of them told me that he could get me anything: "We can arrange anything at all for you," he said in a suggestive tone. Almost all contact with the opposite sex is very restricted in the Muslim-Bangladesh culture. In fact, for weeks I did not talk to a single female, at least not to one who would respond. So, I was not sure what he was referring to. I told him no thanks, that I wanted to sleep.

Boys collecting mud ⊙
for making bricks, a
major export of the
country

Another time, though, it was just too much. I was tired and did not want to be bothered. But within twenty minutes of checking in, I received two calls and three visits from two different boys. On the third visit, the young man asked if there was anything else he could do. I said, "Please, leave me alone. I do not want you knocking on the door." Seconds later, I got a call from the manager asking me if there was a problem. I said no, but that I would appreciate it if the boys would stop knocking on my door; it was annoying. He said he would be right up, hanging up before I had the chance to protest. When he knocked on my door and I opened it, he walked right in—like they all do—and asked me what the problem was. I said I did not want the boys knocking on my door. He said he understood and left. As soon as I was asleep, he called again, this time to assure me that he had directed the boys not to disturb me.

Children ▵

Fruit salesmen ◃

Boat people ▹

The distance from the dock to the ship ready to go up river was about three-hundred feet, so a small boat was used to ferry folks back and forth. This boat would comfortably hold about eight, and I counted forty-three people standing at the pier waiting to get to the ship. The logical thing would be to take two or three trips to get everyone across. This could have been done in a few minutes, but not in Bangladesh! When about thirty people were obviously overloading the tiny, rickety, sixteen-foot craft, various goods and babies (one given to me) were passed to their neighbors to hold above their heads—to move vertically what could not be moved horizontally, to make room for more. This process seemed to take forever. As the weight increased, the rope from the boat tied to the dock was pulled tighter and tighter, until it was so tight it could not be untied. Tugging hard and yelling at the rope by several experts did no good.

Confusion set in, and more time passed until the guy on the dock, deboning chicken for the ship, offered the knife he was using. He cut the filthy rope, and then continued deboning the chicken (without wiping it). Released, the boat, being in shallow water, sank into the mud, and once more we were stuck. After several unsuccessful attempts with the motor at full throttle, some of the passengers finally decided to get out and see if the boat could float with less weight. It did, and the sound of the motor relaxing brought applause. But dropping the passengers off at the anchored ship and returning immediately to retrieve the others was not in anyone's mind. Instead, the barely-floating craft moved to the other side of the dock, where the water was deeper. One at a time, the remaining passengers, balancing carefully, managed to squeeze in, all forty-three or so of us. We finally made it to the ship. Later, the man with the dirty knife finished preparing the spicy chicken for our dinner. (It was delicious.)

< ∨ ∟ ⌐

Most land in the country is only a few feet above sea level, so getting around by boat on the thousands of canals and rivers is the norm.

Tight quarters on board

Rowing with a heavy load for many miles is common.

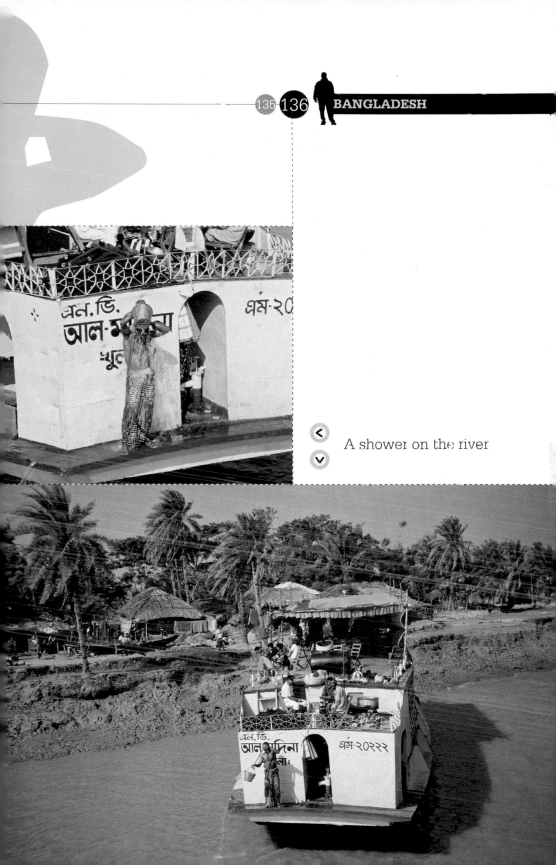

A shower on the river

Getting lost is easy. Local buses cost about three cents, and a trip of hundreds of miles costs only the equivalent of about a dollar. Some are especially uncomfortable, with hard seats, poor suspension, and only one window, in front of the driver. Even so, on one occasion, I managed to fall asleep to the rhythmic jostling. When I woke up, I realized I was far past my destination. I knew where I'd planned to get off because it had been the next big town, but it was now twenty-five minutes past the time we should have been there. The problem was, I had no idea where I was or which way the bus was supposed to go after the town I'd been headed for. I pulled out my compass and confirmed we were going south, definitely not where I wanted to go. To add to the confusion, my map showed no southbound road that made any sense. Naturally, no one on the bus spoke any English nor were the road signs decipherable.

Ⓛ Women dressed in their burkas; little skin is revealed.

I decided I had better get off at the next village and see about how to go back in the other direction. I climbed out of the bus into a mob of women in their full burkas. In Bangladesh, most women show their faces and only about 10 or 20 percent cover all their skin. But in this village, almost no female skin could be seen. Most men had full beards and serious expressions. I, too, had a beard, but it was only about a week old, so it did not make me blend in too well. Some of the men were dead ringers for Osama bin Laden. I took a picture of a few, pretending it was their cooking I was interested in.

I bought some of the flat bread they cooked and went to the other side of the road, hoping a bus in the opposite direction would come by. One did, but it would not stop for me. It was not only full, it had twenty people on the roof and some dangling off the sides. It was a noisy, smoke-billowing contraption that did not look road-worthy. Another went by and another, also overladen. I was starting to feel the kind of feeling anyone might feel when totally lost in a remote village in a remote province of a remote country, not speaking the language or knowing a great deal about the culture. The feeling was not desperation or fear or sadness, it was just being aware of one, overpowering question: "What do I do now?"

The people were usually very helpful, but here they did not know what I needed. Even though it was logical I should go back in the opposite direction from where I had come, there were many forks in the roads and literally thousands of small villages. Most people in Bangladesh live in the countryside, and to find a real city might not be so easy. Would I end up spending the rest of my life walking from village to village?

Then, a man in a purple religious costume who looked
about twenty approached and addressed me in perfect
British English. He was from London, a British-born Bengali
returning to the home of his parents for religious education.
We had a nice chat. I joked about Osama bin Laden look-
alikes and he said many people in the village actually
support him. He explained that virtually all of them are
desperately poor and totally illiterate and have no education
or information, except from the fundamentalist Islamic radio.
They had no clue about international politics and had only
heard that bin Laden was someone who stood up for the
poor and against those who wished to harm Islam, despite
(he added) the facts. He said they were harmless and did
not know any better.

^   Is that Osama bin Laden?

<   Sorting rocks is an example
>   of the ever-present, hard
     manual labor found across
     the country, on the Jamuna
     River.

I wished I could talk more with this interesting guy who
himself had come for the Islamic teaching, but at the
moment I was more interested in finding out where I
was and how to get where I wanted to be. He gave me
directions, and after a short walk, I caught a minibus to
a fantastic little town, this time one on the map, with a
guesthouse that had a satellite dish, CNN on TV, and even
Internet access. I was back on track.

The Sundarbans region of India and Bangladesh includes the largest mangrove forests in the world, with exotic birds, crocodiles, monkeys, and the royal Bengal tiger. When I asked the ranger where to go to see tigers, he told me they were all around. Laughing, he said they help him with the battle against illegal logging. He went on to say that the

only people who spend much time in the forest are honey collectors, and they wear metal helmets covering their heads and necks, not to protect them against bees, but to protect them against tiger attacks. He was not laughing anymore. I followed a trail into the forest, worrying about tigers all the way, but eventually making my way to the southern coast of the Bay of Bengal.

The beach could not have been more inviting, the soft sand separating the ocean from the lush jungle and providing enough open space to relax without fear of tigers. They never attack from the front, I reminded myself, so the danger was far less than when trekking through the dense jungle from where I had come. The spotted deer, the tigers' normal prey, never go to the sand, so the tigers have no reason to be at the beach. After the tense hike through the forest, I

The Sundarbans

was now happily relaxing, listening to the waves breaking peacefully on the gray sand.

Lying back, I was idly noticing how rain had washed away any tracks or footprints and had made some artistic patterns in the sand. But focusing my eyes at a different angle, I realized with a tingle down my spine that I was actually lying on a line of fresh tracks. These were truly giant paw prints, much larger than the ones the ranger had pointed out, and they had to have been made since the rain a few hours before. I whispered a few expletives and grabbed my camera. The peace had vanished. I felt I was being watched, and I peered nervously into the jungle—where I could see only some colorful birds fluttering about.

Spotted deer are the Bengal tigers' favorite food. ⌃

Paw prints from a tiger with nearly-newborn ❯
cub prints alongside at the beach

Paw print larger
than my shoe

I reminded myself that I had been told that the deer, the tigers' preferred food, are plentiful in this area and that there should be little risk to people—but then I had also been told that tigers "never" went on the beach. It also occurred to me that when he went out, the ranger who'd said it was fairly safe always carried a big gun. I decided it was time to move on and started down the beach, trying to stay relaxed, but from time to time, I must admit, looking back nervously over my shoulder.

< Portion of the forest
devastated by the
monsoon

v Sunrise over the Indian
Ocean

< I wedged my camera on a broken tree for a self portrait
where a monsoon has ravaged this formerly heavily
forested area.

INDIA

In Mumbai, I sat in a garden near where the Parsis put their departed to rest. Human corpses are laid out because this faith believes that burning or burying a body is irreverent.

The religions and traditions of India are fascinating, especially in contrast to the modern computer software development and other advanced industry now based there. Hindus worship three main gods, but each of them has 11 million related gods! That is 330 million possible deities to pray to just for Hindus! The worship of several gods at once is common. Many have reverence of cows, and some even rats. And Sikhs, Muslims, Zorastitorians, and many, many other faiths in India all have unique ways to worship. There are men who have themselves surgically castrated to become eunuchs with supposed supernatural powers. Another bizarre religious sect practices public self-mutilation.

I was walking across an intersection and noticed a group of people walking slowly, watching someone. It was a man who was bleeding from his hand and spreading the blood on his chest, all with a trance-like gleam in his eyes. He was carrying a pointed iron rod about a half-inch thick and three feet long. As I watched, he put the end into his mouth sideways and thrust it right through the inside of his cheek until it came out on the outside of his face. I stood there in horror. He seemed to be doing this in some sort of ritual. Soon, fortunately, the police arrived. The officer got his attention, then admonished the man in English, in an understatement: "Aaah, aaah, aaaaah, you should not be doing that."

Three of the 330 million gods are Brahma, Vishun, and Siva.

A whole town carved from one piece of stone

A Mumbai street at night; hundreds of thousands of families are homeless in India.

Detailed stories on many subjects carved into the side of a building

Vegetable Thali, clear evidence that some things taste better than they look.

Muslim prayer tower. There are over 100 million Muslims in India.

▲ Urinals conveniently located on a busy boulevard, flushed only by the rain, in Mumbai

◀ Bangalore is a city with some serious traffic jams.

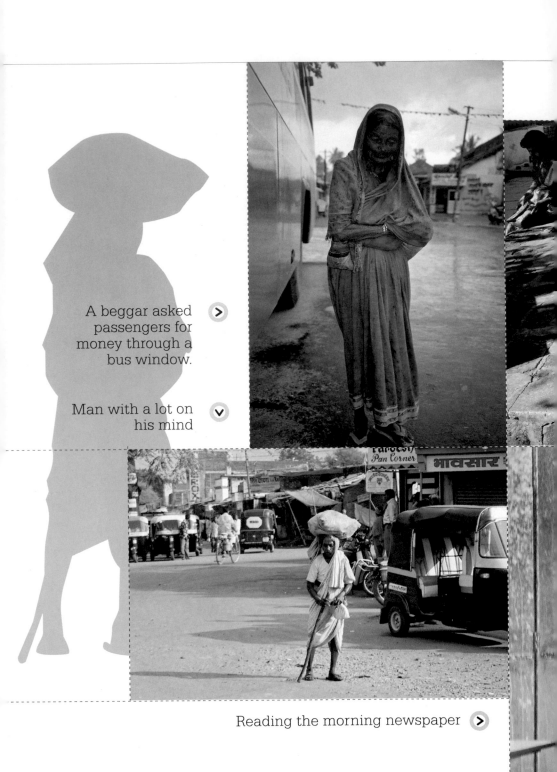

A beggar asked ❯ passengers for money through a bus window.

Man with a lot on ❮ his mind

Reading the morning newspaper ❯

Dad likes to get high. Men are allowed to abandon their families and go on a spiritual journey, often for months at a time, and smoking marijuana regularly is considered acceptable.

MYANMAR

A friend who escorted me through a Burmese temple in Bagan. A school requirement is to adorn the face with powder.

Formerly known as Burma, this country has been under dictatorial military rule for the last decades and the fledgling pro-democracy movement has been violently suppressed. Authorities have tried to prevent foreigners, especially the press, from having any contact with the opposition, making it sometimes difficult for any traveler to obtain a visa. It was the oddest way to get a visa I have experienced.

I have traveled to many countries without any problem, but at Myanmar's embassy in Thailand, instead of someone looking at a computer, collecting a fee, and checking in my passport for pick-up later, they told me first to walk down a hall and sit down inside an office. After a while, in front of this imposing desk stacked with papers, in walked an official who began pacing slowly back and forth. The questioning started. First, he asked how long I had been a journalist. I am not a journalist and told him so, explaining that I work back home as an engineer, in electronics. "Sure, you are a journalist, engineer." When I denied this, he asked for my business card, which I pulled out, feeling relieved that it would surely prove my words. But the conversation continued to go down hill. Why would I be traveling so light, with only a small backpack, if I had no contacts? Why didn't I have an exact itinerary planned? He continued with one provocative question after another, until it seemed clear no visa was going to be issued to me.

Finally, he escorted me to yet another office. There, after a while, a lady politely gave me back my passport—in which she had stamped my visa—and said, "Enjoy our country!"

Buddhist temples of Bagan

Getting around by carriage in Bagan

Kids on their way to school

Getting around town

Beast of burden

Burmese men
wearing their *baso*
in Bagan

◄ ◄ City temple "Su La" in Yangon

◄ ► Buddhist monks

⌄ Minor copyright infringement

JAPAN

Kamuiwakka-yuno-taki,
a hot waterfall at the
Shiretoko-hanto, Hokkaido

My first time in Japan, the budget was so tight that my trip was limited mostly to the countryside, which is far more affordable than travel in cities like Osaka or Kyoto. I was able to stay in cheap rooms in peoples' houses. I ate mostly lunch boxes of pickles and rice, and did a lot of walking. Learning a little of the language, I got by just fine.

Though every schoolchild in Japan takes several years of English, most still have limited foreign language skills. That, along with shyness or embarrassment, makes for few conversations with foreigners. And women and girls of the countryside seem to be especially less brave. On the road, in the north part of Honshu, two in their twenties smiled at me from some distance away and giggled together. After a few minutes, they came closer and, covering their mouths, squeaked with nervous laughter again: "He he hehehe." They seemed to be daring each other to come closer to this foreigner. After a few more steps, the taller one was close enough for me to see fear in her eyes. She took one more look at her friend, then turned her eyes to the ground, seeming to take a deep breath, then brought her eyes up to mine. She had something to say, and it was this: "How... are... you?" They waited with great anticipation for my reply. When I smiled back and answered, "Fine," they giggled with great delight. That was all she needed. Her English had worked.

Shincan sin
bullet train

This
fisherman
would spot
the fish with
mask and
snorkel, then
pop up and
cast his net.

Getting laughed at
for my poor Japanese
pronunciation

More recently, on a family excursion to Japan, hotels and fast trains increased the costs exponentially. One night in Tokyo with dinner and hotel would cost more than $300 U.S.—more than a month's worth of expenses in many other countries. After a few days in glitzy Tokyo, we went up north. Japan's northern island, Hokkaido, is, for the most part, the opposite of the hot and humid, overpopulated, busy central part of the country. The trip from Tokyo to Hokkaido takes all day, but the bullet train averages well over a hundred miles an hour and the scenery is interesting. Toward the end of the journey, the train amazingly goes under water for many miles to reach the island. This was a family trip and Hokkaido is not as well serviced by trains as the rest of Japan, so renting a car was most practical. Driving on the left side of the road was fine—except, of course, when once or twice I forgot.

The plan was to visit as many *onsens* (hot springs) as possible, and they were all over the place. Only a short hike from the road in Akan National Park, paradise was found in the steamy little pools in the midst of the cool alpine forest. In Shiretoko National Park, a peninsula with islands belonging to nearby Russia, we saw deer, interesting birds, and snakes. And there were foxes that were extremely brave who came right up for a sniffing inspection. Searching for another *onsen*, we drove past the end of the paved road and onto a dirt road, all the way to a set of cascades. Most waterfalls here were ice-cold snow run-off, but this one was strangely warm. Hiking up past one cascade after another, the water got warmer and warmer, with several pools along the way to soak in. Finally, at the top, was the hottest one, the bubbling source. Hidden away in a secluded section of this obscure national park on Japan's northern island was this natural jacuzzi: Kamuiwakka-yu-no-taki.

< ^

My family and I looking for an *onsen* (hot spring) in Akan National Park

Eggs cooked in the volcano's sulfur vent had a nice flavor.

Relaxing in a hot bath, my daughter enjoys the good life in a youth hostel in Akan National Park.

Hokkaido
farmers ⌃

Farm ❯

‹

My daughter
is face to face
with the fierce
Hokkaido
stuffed bear.

‹ ⌄

Hokkaido fox

In the city, a capsule hotel seems strange the first time you stay in one. This spa-like place in Sapporo had high-tech lockers on the ground floor just for shoes, which are forbidden on the eight floors above. Down the hall, there were two elevators: one for women, one for men. The capsule rooms were literally the size of a small bed, with the ceiling barely three feet above the sleeping surface. They were stacked in rows, with a ladder to each one-person capsule. Like an ultra-luxurious dormitory room with a TV and other amenities molded into the plastic ceiling and walls, it was actually quite comfortable, once one managed to wiggle into bed.

Baths in Japan are for relaxing. You start in a special room with little cubicles full of fresh razors, disposable toothbrushes, various soaps, and shampoos. Sitting on a tiny stool, you must wash well, and then the fun begins. About fifteen different areas are ready for you to unwind in. First, there is the one-person-at-a-time tub, contoured to the body; then in a separate area, a high-end bubble machine; and then, after fifteen minutes or so, the quiet room, where you simply sit in comfortable lounge chairs in near darkness. It felt strange at first, but peace seemed to waft out of the walls and—what was that smell, that very good smell? Next was a shallow pool made from dark granite, big enough for fifty people and not very hot; what made it so relaxing was the combination of the pleasant aroma and the darkness. In another room, a high-definition TV and great acoustics provided an entirely different form of relaxation. Sometimes, there were a lot of people in one of the areas, but no one interfered with the peace and quiet of others. Even my 6'4" relatively pale body attracted little attention.

Next, there were two different kinds of very hot saunas: first dry for a time, then steamy. These were followed by two symmetrical cold waterfalls flowing over you. The feeling at this point was absolute pleasure; not a thought was in my brain, except that of never wanting to leave. Of the other stations, the best was last: an outdoor place where everything was made of wood, including an amazing very hot bath about 15 x 30 feet with high walls and carved corners. The cold air balanced the hot water, and soaking there, outdoors on the balcony, was great. This entire experience took about two hours; after a good night's sleep, it was time to get up and do the whole process over again.

Spa capsule hotel in Sapporo, Hokkaido

∧ Getting prettied up   ↘ Washing stool

∨ Very hot bath   ↵ Even the toilet is fancy. This one cleans and dries one's backside automatically.

GHANA

Less expensive than most countries are those of West Africa, where just about everything is remarkably affordable. A train ticket to go hundreds of miles costs less than $6 U.S. But the best deal was a dormitory-style hotel, where I was given my own private room anyway. The room was fine, the water was hot, the facilities were clean, and the staff was very friendly. The price was about $4 U.S. a week, or 71 cents a day. The manager also said he would negotiate a better rate for a longer stay.

In West Africa, there is no shortage of fashionable hairdos.

‹ Humorous sign

⌄ Busy street scene in Accra

Western missionaries have had a significant effect on culture in Africa. Here, a sign on a Christian clinic advertises an herbal remedy promising a cure for a number of diseases, including AIDS.

For a little more money, one can get very nice accommodations indeed. One place had its own compound with a security wall around it. It wasn't that there was actually any danger; it just gave a feeling of extra safety for the upscale clientele, which temporarily included me. It only had eight or ten rooms, with art on the walls and plants everywhere. I was given the fancy front unit near the garden.

I was comfortable in bed, feeling especially impressed with the new friends I'd met that day, until I was woken up by the noise of some men outside the compound. There seemed to be about twenty or thirty of them, all yelling and making terrible sounds, sort of like a football team rallying after an angry pep talk: Ug uug auag. It got louder and some women joined in. This was no football lingo. They were obviously angry at something, and one person in the group was screaming in rage. As the sounds got louder, I got frightened. They had managed to get into the compound and were right outside my window. They kept chanting, but I had no clue what it was about.

I do not scare easily, nor am I naive about danger; nevertheless, I was terrified. I was the only foreigner of any kind I had seen for several days. After about forty-five minutes of standing ready to be raided, Swiss Army knife blade open, I could tell that at last they had quieted down and left. I opened my door and looked out, still shaken up. No one was around. Eventually, I went back to sleep. In the morning, I asked the manager what the commotion was about. He explained that a man and woman had a relationship but their families did not approve; the couple had sought refuge in the compound. In other words, it was all a Romeo-and-Juliet sort of thing. He apologized for the disturbance. Since I had not met a single person who had been unfriendly anywhere in the region, I now felt inwardly embarrassed for imagining that I might be a target.

Lively street on market day

Going topless is
not uncommon in
West Africa.

For a few dollars,
you can go
hundreds of
miles in these old
German trains in
central Ghana.

Exploring at the beach, I came to an old slave fort, where slaves had been held before being shipped to the new world. It had been turned into a museum and memorial, a sad place to visit with many chambers where two centuries before, humans were treated worse than animals. There were relics all around that would give anyone reason for sad thoughts. Cannons were still in position, instruments used by the Portuguese, Dutch, and other white men who were fighting each other for control of the lucrative slave business. As I imagined the awful reality of what had happened there, I couldn't help but notice that the predominant centerpiece of the European slave traders' fort was a Christian church.

⌄ Slave fort, Ghana

Cannons were still in position at a slave fort.

Crammed, sometimes hundreds at a time, into small rooms, the soon-to-be slaves had no toilets or adequate food. Captives were sometimes held for months waiting for the next ship. Now, only bats occupy these rooms.

The cannons next to me were used by white men fighting other white men for control of the slave fort.

Chambers for female slaves

There is no such thing as a new car in much of West Africa. Most cars are five to ten years old and in poor condition when purchased. A lower-end Peugeot that's considered to have come to the end of its useful life in Europe will often end up in Africa. Because simple transportation is all that is needed, the car is first stripped. Anything not necessary for mobility is sold off, sometimes even the headlights and bumpers. The entire dash panel is often missing, including the speedometer, warning lights, seat belts, and horn; even keys and ignition are replaced with a switch.

Taking a taxi in the region is always an experience, but one particular ride was especially memorable. The owner had reduced his car to the barest of bones; even the seats had been replaced with some uncomfortable, homemade wooden ones. This guy had not even replaced the missing key and ignition with a switch-he'd just connected two bare wires together to hot-wire it. It even sounded as if some major engine components were missing, too, and the car was constantly stalling.

But he had a solution. He wrapped one of the wires around his thumb and the other around his index finger. Then, every time the car would stall, which was often, he would restart it with his fingers. Since a lot of current goes to the starter motor, he would get an electric shock each time he touched the wires together. His body would jump and he would grimace with pain. It was more than I could take. Giving him a little extra in tip as I got out, I told him, "Please use this money to buy a switch."

A huge hydroeloctric facility at Akosombo Dam on Lake Volta-but power priority is given to a foreign-owned aluminum factory. I heard of this when the owner of the hotel next to it explained why his electricity was so sporadic. I took my bath by lantern light.

There is almost no limit to what can be balanced on one's head in West Africa.

Ladies on the way to market in eastern Ghana

A bush taxi is one that goes out of a town and into the bush, or countryside. I wanted to visit a remote village perched on a mountain ridge and negotiated with some drivers to take me there. I should have taken warning when the first six taxis refused the job. Normally here, anyone will accept any job for reasonable pay.

One guy said OK—for enough money. The cost was relatively high, something like $6 U.S. The rocky dirt road would have been difficult even for a four-wheel drive, with dips in the road bigger than the car. Zigzagging up the mountain, this vehicle was definitely taking a beating and so was my backside. After a couple of hours averaging only about five miles per hour, I was in pain and it was too dark for him to go further, at least without working headlights. He said he needed to turn back. How he would make it back in the dark without going off the cliff was one question; where I would be going in the dark, by foot in a remote corner of nowhere, was another. We exchanged wishes of "good luck," and I continued up the road, where he'd said I couldn't miss the village.

Alone in the dark, it was spooky. And after a while it got more so, when I heard a faint drum beat. This is the real Africa, I thought. It got louder and I glimpsed a flicker of firelight far off in the darkness. I turned my flashlight off, and under the black night sky I headed toward the only light besides the stars, the fire in the distance. Getting closer, I heard singing accompanying the drumbeat. Closer still, I saw the silhouettes of more than a hundred people who were dancing, circling around the large fire. Everyone there was a participant; there was no separate audience—except for me.

What with the music and dancing, and only the fire for light, no one noticed me for a while. Finally, a young man in shorts did spot me. He was surprised but managed to convey that the chief would want to speak to an unexpected visitor. The chief was dancing, too. Or at least he was in the midst of it all. He and some of his wives eventually came over to me and he introduced himself. He had the demeanor of a powerful man. If I understood him right, he said he was a university graduate. He welcomed me and indicated where I could sleep.

The next morning, I ate something for breakfast that may have been eggs, though not from a chicken, then left to explore the length of the ridge, where I found some other villages. There, everyone was even more surprised to see an outsider. It was like being a celebrity. Kids would run ahead, and when I got to a group of huts, greeters made me feel more welcome each time. One man talked to me about their religion, Juju; he had a lot to say and was friendly, but he made a quick joke about the high value of a white man's head. He shared his fruit and was especially nice to me, so I am 99 percent sure that his remark was just a joke.

Jungle in Kujani National Park

> Some bush meat showed up on my doorstep.

Trekking through the jungle is just about my favorite thing to do. Though happy and fascinated in a West African rain forest, at one point I got a little lost. The trail was faint and seemed to have forked a few times, so it was not clear which way I should go next. I had seen some people along the way, but hesitated to approach, never having asked naked people for directions before. But soon, realizing I needed some help, I went ahead. The guy I approached had a primitive look about him but broke out in a big smile upon seeing a foreigner. I asked him which way to the village and he explained in clear English. (Ghana was formerly a British colony, so English is widely spoken.) He asked where I was from and when I said America, his expression immediately turned serious. "Leave Clinton alone," he admonished. This was during the time when the story of the former U.S. president's affair was dominating the news. He exclaimed, "It is his own private matter! Leave him alone!" I nodded my head, not disagreeing with him, and started to speak.

But he was not listening. He said he had heard the whole thing on the radio, had followed it closely, and could not understand Americans. "Please leave him alone! It is a private matter, you see!" He continued past me, conveying aloofness and disapproval in his posture.

The nicest people in the world may live in Ghana. Even in the jungle, most spoke to me in English, so I went to the national playhouse in the capital of Accra to see a show, expecting it to be in English. But I soon realized it was being performed in one of the local dialects. When everyone laughed at the first words, I felt a little left out. Then some people around me shuffled and changed seats, and next thing I knew, a woman—a total stranger to me—began whispering into my ear. She translated throughout the whole play for me, making it come to life. She did not speak except for translating, and when the show ended, she quickly got up and went back to her group.

A play in Accra's national playhouse

Coconut salesmen near Ada

Everything is eaten with the fingers in West Africa, even hot stew!

This is how people are in Ghana. They want to help, offering kindness at every turn. People with nothing would offer food or friendly conversation, always with smiles and a sense of fun and curiosity about this foreigner. I met a girl at the beach where there were some food stalls. She and I talked for a time and I was impressed with her intelligence. I felt as if I had met her on a university campus, with our conversation quickly turning to serious topics such as economics. Then, she needed to get something from her purse, and suddenly I saw more about the realities of her life. Her purse was a plastic one, like a four-year-old American would play with. The snap was broken and the triangular mirror was broken, too; some cloth, dog-eared paper, a stub of a pencil, and a stick for brushing her teeth were all that was inside. I then noticed her clothes had holes in them. Many people looked like this, but she was so intelligent, I was still shocked by how little she obviously had. She was living in a hut at the beach with her family. She was desperately poor, owning nothing more than those ragged clothes on her back and a toy purse. Yet she said nothing about having a hard life during our conversation. Her job was to pick up trash at the food stalls and maybe get some scraps to eat at the end of the day. She was beautiful and very smart and wanted nothing from me except conversation.

West Africa has endless beautiful beaches.

Preparing some dinner near Kumasi

I made friends with another woman at the fish market. She came from Liberia. Our conversation also became deep quickly, and I was impressed with her calm and maturity, especially considering her age—late teens—and what she was telling me. She spoke about her escape from that war-torn country. She said the fighters controlling the area they had to cross were very brutal; to intimidate people, they forced anyone passing by the checkpoint to kiss the enemy's cut-off heads stuck on poles along the roads. She said that was not the worst thing; they were starving as they left, eating only grass and getting water from the dew on the plants in the mornings. She said her baby barely survived, but should now be safe with her parents. But she had not seen her baby in more than a year.

⌃ Lively marketplace, Kumasi

There was a restaurant near the port, but the region was so poor they had little food on hand, just *fufu* (prepared cassava), some other vegetables, and spices. When I sat down, the man gave me a menu that looked good, but he explained that I would have to walk a little way to the port to get what I wanted to eat, and then they would cook it. I came back with a fine lobster. They prepared it, and I ate a first-class meal with great vegetables, an amazing lobster, and palm wine. This exquisite meal cost me about $3 U.S.

Fishermen repairing nets ⌃

Fish on head ↰

A pig enjoying a day at the beach; I passed by the potential pork chops and went for the lobster instead. ❯

A gas station in
West Africa with low
overhead

A gas station is often nothing but a hodgepodge of large
bottles, plastic containers, and odd shaped buckets full of
fuel. Underground tanks would be too expensive. The long-
distance minivan stopped for gas. Even though I loved the
popular Nigerian music the driver had playing on the stereo,
I was glad to get out to stretch my legs. The van could
have comfortably carried maybe six adults and luggage; on
this trip, it was holding more than twenty people, several
goats, chickens, and some other animals croaking loudly
in the back. After the fill-up, we passengers were happy to
get back in, because even though we'd all been strangers
at first, we'd become friends, laughing and listening to the
great music. The unbelievably tight conditions bothered no
one. It was a rolling party.

Cramped van; long-distance transportation in West Africa is always fuller than full.

Cheap hotel made from mud, straw, and palm leaves.

< Bus station with no full-sized buses; instead, vans are jammed to the max with people and cargo.

⌄ This taxi was one of the fanciest around.

You know a place is poor when the police department traffic division has no vehicles, and speeding citations are written by officers on foot. But poor does not mean stupid. Many roads have gates that are quickly lowered before unsuspecting violators. An officer on the phone with a spotter a mile before calculates the speed with synchronized watches and the known distance the vehicle had traveled. The average speed is precisely determined. There is no point to argue; the officers did the math.

TOGO

Sky and trees full of bats in Lome, the capital of Togo

Canoes for rent by a woman letting it all hang out

The sky in Togo's capital of Lome was full of thousands of bats. These were not the familiar small nocturnal bats, but very large fruit bats that had no problem making themselves visible in daylight. I had just passed through a mess of border crossings, including one where I had to bribe one official to get to the next one who was actually waiting eagerly to stamp my passport. (If you go to Africa, get extra passport pages for the stamp-happy border guards.) There were other difficulties, too, so I was not in a good mood. The French-speaking locals were hardly friendly, not even the bare-breasted women; I felt more welcomed by the bats.

I decided to go to the zoo, which was an agreeable enough place. Developing countries often have simple zoos of caged animals; at least this place had tall trees and my cousins were there—some very cool-looking monkeys. But the residents of the cages were, for the most part, less interesting than the creatures in the trees above the zoo; that was a spot where the wild bats congregated.

The cheap hotel where I slept was no less interesting and had bats, too. As I walked up the stairs, a smaller bat flew by; I spotted another in the corner of the stairwell. My room, though, was bat-free, and having seen enough for one day, I closed the wide-open window to keep it that way.

BENIN

In Grand Marche de Dantokpa, this voodoo shaman said I could not take his picture directly, but a picture of his picture was alright.

Skulls, tails, and fetish carvings; the two black figurines on the left now sit on my bookshelf.

Voodoo originated in Benin, so I paid a visit to a juju priest to see the traditional religion of West Africa in action. Hundreds of animal skulls were displayed on tables in a large, open-air area like a market. All shapes and sizes were there, from reptiles to birds and dogs, and spooky monkey skulls that looked almost human; there were fresh furry heads, too. All were frightening images, used for their supposed magical powers to put a hex on someone or remove one. People would also come if they were sick or just looking for some good luck. My understanding was that the priest would spit gin on them and go into a frenzy to get the magic going.

I was offered some expensive treatment. It took him twenty minutes to explain some of the nuances of the magical powers, but I said I had no problems and did not need any help. Even though I told him I just wanted to buy a woodcarving, he did not understand how that could be. When I pointed at the one I wanted, and ended up buying, he became upset, yelling "No powers at all! No powers at all!"

Skulls that include a fresh dog's head

Skulls and carved idols used for their
believed supernatural powers. Costs for
their use include the full ritual of casting
or removing a hex, disease, or good luck.

Canoeists in a coastal village

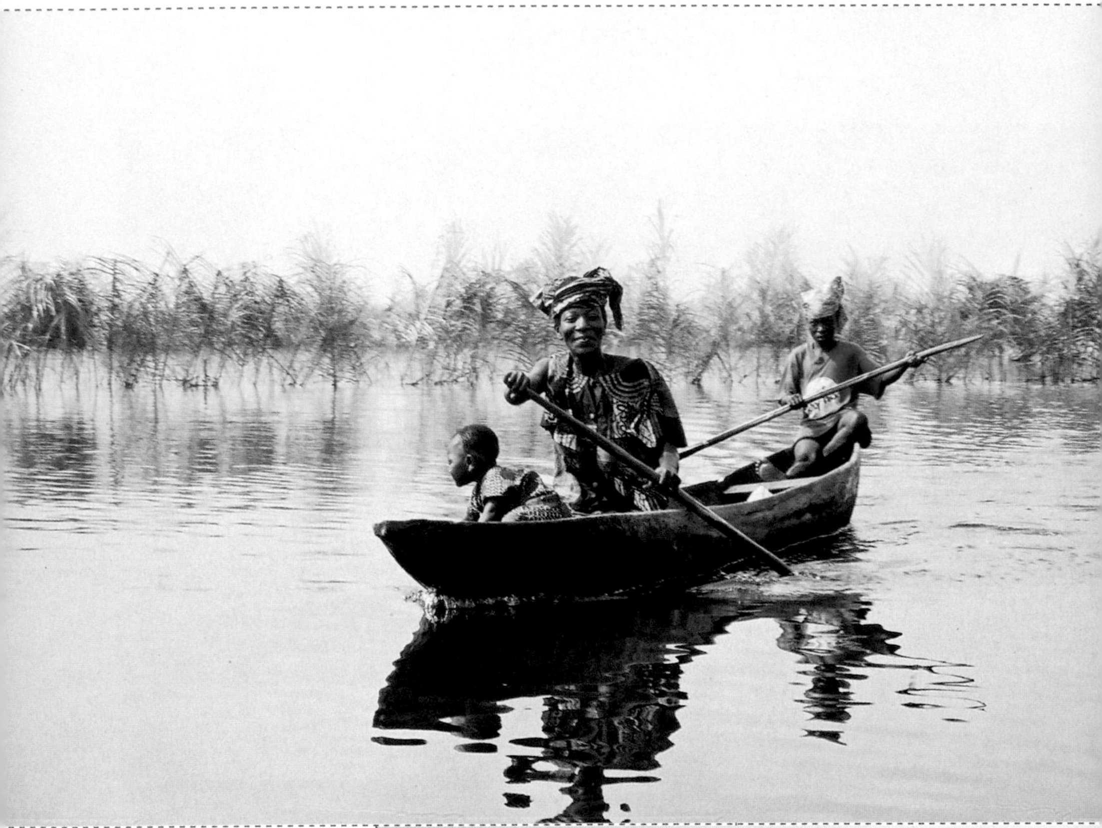

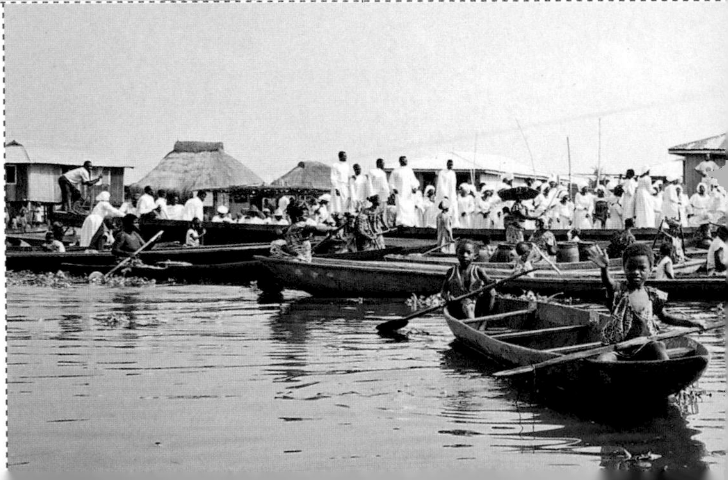

An entire town without land near Ganvie; this fishing village in Benin could be a problem for sleepwalkers!

RUSSIA

Train station on the Trans-Siberian Express Railway

The longest train ride in the world, nearly six thousand miles, may also be the most enjoyable. Eastward from Europe to the Pacific Coast, the Trans-Siberian Railway is a seemingly endless visual masterpiece. Winter in Siberia sounds ominous, with visions of the gulags of the former Soviet Union, but from the comfort and warmth of a train car, beauty is what I saw. The warmth of the people traveling the great distance was also exceptional. To meet a foreigner was a reason for many to celebrate, and impromptu parties abound. Trying to communicate could be a challenge, but my hundred or so words of Russian went a long way with friendly people. One of the parties, if you could call it that, was different than the others. Two older men, who had melancholy written on their faces, gestured if I would like to drink with them.

I sat down, and a bottle of vodka was pulled out of an old cloth sack and opened; the cap, tossed away. He put three small cups on the table with no ice or other dilutants. The husky red-nosed men and I finished the room-temperature vodka, and hardly a word was spoken. Drinking did not seem fun for them but a kind of serious business. No obvious drunkenness, no smiles, no apparent mood alteration at all, just something they seemed to need and probably did every day of their lives. Though their kindness was clear and a toast to "peace" was done twice, this experience was a bit sad to me as an example of how all too many Russians lived their lives.

Mongolian ⌃
yurt

Mongolian ❯
camels

Simple Siberian beauty

Horse-drawn sled in the desolation of central Siberia

Individual train cabins are supplied with fresh
heather and tea offerings daily.

My first visit to Siberia, back in the summer of 1984, was
during communist rule. Stern-faced soldiers guarding the
train station examined the trickle of tourists entering the
Soviet Union. Some passengers were singled out to go into
a private room for a closer examination. I was one chosen.
Once the door was shut and his superiors were out of sight,
the young soldier smiled and half-pretended to search in the
top of my pack, giving it less than a two-second glance. He
then sat down, and with laziness about him, put his feet on
the other seat and relaxed. My first evidence of one of the
principles of workers in the country: "They pretend to pay
us and we pretend to work." (Sarcastic political thoughts
like that would be measured in how many years in prison
you would serve for saying it. A truly hilarious comment
poking fun at the ills of communism would be considered
a ten-year joke.) After a while, those outside would think a
thorough examination had been performed. When sufficient
time had passed, he painted the fierce look back on his face
and opened the door.

Looking at
Siberia's
beauty

Moscow
images near
the Kremlin

Catching
the ballet in
Moscow

Soviet statue usually means big; note the size of the truck on the right.

Lake Baykal near Irkutsk

Meals in the Soviet Union were often delicious, but not because of any variety of ingredients; instead, the amazing resourcefulness of the cooks was evident. The best example was on the train going east. Leaving the western part of Russia, the meals were quite tasty, but as the train passed through central Asia, the food began to run out and fewer and fewer selections were offered in the dining car. In the final few days approaching the Pacific Ocean, I was amazed again and again at what could be done with only cucumbers and potatoes.

I enjoy a glass of *kvas*, a light brew made from bread pumped from a truck; it was served in a glass that was not washed but instead was wiped out with a dirty towel before being given to the next customer in a long line.

Sitting in front of some classic propaganda posters; this American appropriately chose a red, white, and blue bench.

Contradiction
in technology: a
museum display of
Sputnik, the first
human-delivered
satellite; while below,
this steam-powered
train was still in use
in the USSR.

Bikini bathers
working on their tans;
a surprising find at a
remote lake in Siberia

Forest

I take a walk in a forest to hunt for mushrooms.

Strange as it may seem, Siberia was and still is a very popular place for summer vacations, especially for those wanting to collect wild mushrooms. I met a family from Moscow who had come to do just that. They invited me along for an afternoon in the forest. No stranger to hiking, I took my bearings and set out thinking I could surely go farther than these significantly overweight people and get the most mushrooms.

There really were a variety to choose from, and in a short time, I'd picked a good collection. There were fat ones, skinny ones, black, white, purple, and slimy ones, both hands full. When we all met up, they, too, had many mushrooms and they looked to the *babushka* (grandmother) to cook them in a simple butter sauce. Before indicating I could share in their tasty, edible mushrooms, and ordering me, "Wash your hands," she'd received and began preparing everyone else's mushrooms. But she laughed somewhat harshly at my collection. The father shook his head, "Nyet nyet nyet," and divided my assortment into several different piles. "None you can eat," he pronounced. Pointing at the first group, in his deep voice and broken English he said, "This one kill you!" Indicating the next group, he exclaimed, "These kill you, too." Then he got to the last group: "These make you violently ill."

Collecting mushrooms is
a major national pastime
in Russia. Without
knowledge, it can become
a deadly hobby.

  Siberian villages near Novosivirsk

ECUADOR

Somewhere over Central America

Ecuador is a small country, but it is very diverse in terrain. My climb to conquer the Tungurahua volcano, up over 15,000 feet, began at 2 a.m. This was so I could make the trek of several hours up to the peak before the sun would soften the snow and make the descent, by foot, too dangerous. Once back down, I got on a small bus, and later, a bigger bus. At one point, the passengers, including me, of course, had to push this bus through a muddy stretch of road in the rain. Already tired from the morning's climb, I was totally worn out by this, but the views approaching the Amazon were amazing. Within only a few hours, the scenery had changed from snow-capped peaks above the clouds, down through several distinct ecological zones, to the flora and fauna of the beginning of the largest rainforest on earth.

Excited about being near the Amazon basin for the first time and up for another hike, I started down a trail and quickly found a spot that looked suitable for a nap. But a large, unfamiliar bug on my ear awoke me after a few minutes, and other creepy crawlers nearby were unsettling; no sleep here. Walking further, I was startled by some strange rodents that looked like giant rats. I stepped over a large chenopod, and spiders were dangling everywhere—especially right in front of me at eye level. Further up the trail, army ants (or something similar) had occupied an entire large tree. Then I encountered more thick mud to trudge through—so thick that going even a short distance was very difficult. Finally, I got to the small town with its modest hotel. The insects were still thick in the air. Totally exhausted from climbing the peak that morning, pushing the bus, and trekking through the jungle, I just wanted to get some rest. Staggering inside, seeing an amazing variety of insects whether my eyes were open or shut, I inquired at the desk and got assurance about only one amenity before taking a room: window screens.

MEXICO

Palenque is a city in southern Mexico where local Mayan ruins, forests, and Indian culture are close by to see and explore, and the small town has real charm. But life is slow here. The first day, I walked by several locals on the street selling homemade dolls. They sat there almost as still as the goods they were selling, seeming to sit in the same place for hours. That evening, walking past to get some dinner, I noted that their positions had not changed.

Three days later, I returned after a jungle trip and they were still in the same positions. I decided to say hi, half wondering if they were real people. I asked, what's happening: "Que paso?" The man I addressed replied, nearly motionless, with one word that nothing was happening: "Nada."

Pyramid in Chichen Itza, Yucatan

Beginning the journey through the Copper Canyon ⌃

Yours truly getting a well-needed bath, Agua Azul. ❯

⌃ Beautiful Agua Azul cascades, Chiapas

⌃ Indian girl

EXPLORING EUROPE

My first trips abroad were mostly exploring Europe. These one- to three-month adventures were separated by long stretches of anticipating the next chance to get on the road again. While stuck at home, I lived as frugally as possible and saved a good percentage of my meager income for future travel. Those first excursions were always on an extremely low budget; on some I spent only a few hundred dollars total, did not take a camera, and even slept outside homeless-style a number of times. I remember being rudely awakened by grass sprinklers turning on in a London park.

There was one fellow traveler from Hungary, though, who was on an even tighter budget. We met in Sweden. At that time, the Hungarian government was the only Eastern European country allowing its citizens to travel west, so he was there, but he had not been allowed to take any money with him. He was traveling to many of the same countries as I, but all on his bicycle, sleeping outside, carrying all his food with him, all the way from Hungary! Naturally enough, he desperately wanted to trade some of his canned sardines for whatever anyone else had that was edible.

DENMARK

At Copenhagen's Tivoli amusement park, it was time to relax and just see the people go by. Two teenaged girls sat down on either side of me on the bench, speaking Danish. Then one opened her umbrella and positioned it above me. Wondering what was going on, I said I was sorry, I did not understand. One of them then asked in English, "Do you think it is going to rain?"

Catching on, I replied, "There is hardly a cloud in the sky," and they laughed. This had been their way to make friends, and we talked for a while. They lived on an island on the other side of Denmark and had taken a boat and train to the amusement park to escape boredom. We spent some time together walking around, and they were playful and as sweet as could be. They invited me to one of their homes to stay a few days. I wanted to, but thought I had better not. They were a bit too flirtatious for being only fifteen!

FINLAND

My first day in Helsinki, Finland, I needed to exchange currency and asked a man on the street where I could find a bank. He turned and walked in my direction to make sure I found the way, not an unusual gesture for Europeans. We exchanged a few questions, and when we approached the bank, he asked why I needed to get money—I was a guest in his country. It seemed a strange comment to me, but he seemed sincere and went on to say that we needed to pick up his wife and his daughter so we could all do something fun. With some hesitation, I followed. We found his family and proceeded to a restaurant for a delicious dinner of reindeer steaks. I offered to pay, but he said I was crazy, repeating that it was their country and I was a guest. We went to another place, where we listened to jazz and drank a caraway-seed beverage. He was a butcher and she an aspiring actress; both very fun-loving people. We partied through the evening and had a great time. I was amazed that they would spend their entire week's pay just to have fun with a stranger for an evening. They took me by taxi back to where I wanted to stay, and as we were all saying goodbye, he said he hoped I had a good first impression of their country. It was hard to tell him just how good that impression was.

YUGOSLAVIA

A bus trip of fourteen grueling hours through the mountains of southern Yugoslavia started happily enough with men laughing in the back. There were Serbs, Croats, and Macedonians on board, but no restroom. The driver would not stop, except for one very short food break for himself. There was not sufficient time for passengers to both get some food and use the facilities—just enough to wait in one long, slow line for a disgusting toilet or to wait in another long, slow line for equally smelly food. Those not back on the bus in time would be left behind. As hours again went by, there was some discussion on this lower-class bus about the driver not stopping for any restroom breaks or food. There was apparently some reason why people would not ask him to stop, possibly ethnic tension. Finally, there was some smoke from the engine and the driver pulled over. He got out, and behind him every soul on the bus followed. Women went to the left side of the bus to relieve themselves, and on the right side we thirty-five men and boys positioned ourselves along the edge of the mountain road, an amusing sight as we all urinated in unison.

HUNGARY

In Hungary, I was with a guy and two girls and we decided to go out to drink beer. The small table in a dark cafe quickly became crowded with empty bottles. I said I did not want to drink any more until eating something, so they ordered the house special. We ate most of it quickly, not worrying about the taste, just concentrating on getting something in our stomachs. It was a piece of thick, dry bread with a layer of some white stuff and a slice of onion, heavily sprinkled with paprika. When asked if it was good, I nodded yes, but inquired what the half-inch layer of white substance was. The man replied, "zsiros kenyer," which of course meant nothing to me. After a few more beers, though, he remembered what it is called in English: "Ah yes, pure lard."

AUSTRIA

The view of the hills nearby were beautifully reminiscent of the movie The Sound of Music. Sitting high up on the wall of a romantic medieval castle, a new friend and I joined others eating bread and fancy cheese. An American backpacker remarked as to how advanced and sophisticated most of Europe seemed to be. Exploring around the grand hallways and peering out through the thick open windows brought me to imagine what it would have been like to be there hundreds of years before. A local expert was on hand for a talk about the Inquisition, then on to a tour of some hidden rooms below. Imprinted in my mind now forever are horrible images of the torture chamber. A stretching machine designed to pull the limbs from sockets of living people or to break the back, lengthening one's body slowly. Other devices were used to impale the victim who would slide down a beam on their own weight. Not puncturing any vital organs, it was designed to allow victims to suffer, sometimes for days. We could hear the echoes of the screams from long ago. With giant screws and hooks for hanging people on the walls, and the variety of other instruments present, none would seem to quickly put someone out of their misery. Europe had not always been so refined.

NORWAY

Norway may, on the whole, have the most spectacularly beautiful landscape on earth. One spring, when I was hitchhiking south from Voss (mid-south) to the southern tip of the country, the fjords and snow-capped mountains were so stunning that I pulled my hitcher's thumb in several times, preferring to be out in the open. The sky was a clear blue; walking on a road through endless forests with meadows full of wildflowers, there was a kaleidoscope of color and waterfalls as numerous as the people. Reaching the edge of a fjord, I met up with a fellow going my way in one of the many Volvos in that country. After crossing the water on a ferry and heading up into the mountains, we went into a tunnel. Coming out the other side of the mountain, we were suddenly blinded by a whiteout, a blizzard. Snow covered everything. With poor visibility and ice on the roads, he carefully drove down the mountain; then we caught a ferry across another fjord. Then up again, into another tunnel, and out the other side of this mountain— where blue sky magically appeared once again.

Another guy I met hitchhiking was especially nice, and we had a great chat. We got along so well, in fact, that he wanted to take me to his home in this beautiful but isolated area and introduce me to his daughter. When he remarked that I'd make a nice son-in-law, though, I got cold feet.

SWITZERLAND

Driving the German Autobahn was fun, speed being limited only by the power of the vehicle and the sanity of the driver. Soon in Switzerland, the fast mountain roads were banked very steeply. Then life slowed down abruptly at the Stoos ski resort. A horse-drawn carriage escorts to accommodations right on the ski slope. Stoos is a romantic and very peaceful place, with mostly locals on the slopes. People in the village sip the local libation, schnapps, and always greet one another with a friendly *grüetzi*. One ski run is so long that it requires rest breaks while skiing down- pure paradise for a good skier. And with the rooms right on the slope, the only footwear necessary for this holiday were ski boots. After a pleasurable week of deep powder, it was back to Germany where the pace quickly picked up again going well over 100 miles per hour on the Autobahn. I thought we were going very fast, until a Porsche zoomed by like we were standing still.

GERMANY

The German North Sea has many good places to have a holiday. Amrum is an island where you can drink some unusual well water that tastes more like seawater than fresh, but it is drinkable. Historically, the sick would be sent to the island for rest and recovery. I guess they would rest, since this strange mineral water has the effect of making you very sleepy, possibly due to the high iodine content. It was certainly a relaxing place. The beaches seem like the edge of the world. Sand grass dancing in the wind keeps the island from blowing away, and cottages have thatched roofs looking just as they have for hundreds of years. The island itself was altogether beautiful and so were many of the nude sunbathers.

U.S.A.

It was not long ago that a simple request to a flight attendant could grant a passenger access to the cockpit in-flight for a visit with the pilot and a look out the front window. I took this photo at 30,000 feet.

Vacations are important to most people, but to me my journeys are perhaps more of a religious experience than vacation. These trips are enormously important to my being. In fact, a mild depression often haunts me when not traveling for some time. The diagnosis is acute chronic reverse homesickness, I guess. The cure is clear, but to relieve symptoms in the short term I have learned to deal with this odd condition by playing tricks on myself.

I'll pretend I am on the road far away by taking public transportation even if driving my car is more practical or go alone to a local museum or ethnic restaurant. Some years ago, I would go to the airport sometimes and just sit.

After a trip across Asia in 1984, I was back home only a few weeks, feeling sad that the seven weeks abroad couldn't have been longer. So, I decided to go over to LAX after work, check on the price of a flight, and sit at an airport lounge and people-watch awhile, sort of pretending to myself I was still on a trip. Despite the obvious pitfalls of communism, the Soviet Union had been absolutely fascinating and the Russian culture had really worn off on me. At the airport, with that trip still on my mind, I mumbled to myself in a Russian accent. Having heard Russian for so many days, I did a pretty good imitation and decided to try it out on a stranger. Near the counter, a man with bad breath asked me something and I responded with an imaginative but convincing story about my fictitious Russian motherland.

Deception is not my usual style, but inside I was laughing hysterically at the good acting job I was doing. I started out of the terminal until, noticing the Travelers' Aid booth, I inquired about a map—still with the accent. The white-haired lady was helpful and then asked where I was from. "Moscow," I told her, and spontaneously continued in broken English, "I doing research on Americans." She asked about a specific Russian city, and with my recent visit, I was able to talk in detail about it. She was convinced, too! Thanking her, I continued out of the airport, giggling about my antics and promising myself not to be silly like that again.

This was long before terrorism frightened so many Americans; instead, communism was the threat. On the long walkway out to the parking lot, a police officer appeared, approached me, and said, "Excuse me, would you mind waiting a minute?" I dropped my accent—quick. Within minutes, I was surrounded by a group of uniformed officers and FBI agents in business suits, maybe fifteen in all. They asked to see my passport more than ten times, which I did not have; each time, I repeated that I was just in the airport for a drink, explaining over and over in different words that I was not from abroad, I was just a local checking on the price for a flight. They took me voluntarily to the airport police station, where I was interrogated for more than an hour. They would not say why I was being held, just repeated a variety of questions, including the names of my grade-school teachers. Other questions were also humorous, but some were starting to get intimidating.

I guess that the Travelers' Aid lady must have turned in what she thought was a secret agent. And after years with the Cold War raging but not finding many Soviet spies, the authorities thought they had finally found one—and it was me! And I guess what helped convince them was my long hair and dirty motorcycle jacket. They treated me in a very professional way, but walking past the interrogation-room window was a continual parade of what seemed to be officers wanting to get a glimpse of their first captured Russian spy. On one hand, this was wildly entertaining, but I was also starting to wonder how long I would be detained.

Finally, after one of my answers, the lead interrogator grinned and shook his head downward. He'd finally accepted that I was, in fact, who my driver's license said I was. I was escorted to the parking lot, where the officers examined my motorcycle. Finding nothing alarming, they half-apologized, but warned me not to return to the airport unless I was going someplace.

Soviet freighter unloading in the Hong Kong harbor

On the bike that took me across the U.S.A.,
I pose at the southernmost point of the
continental U.S., Key West, Florida.

It was a remote part of eastern Texas in the middle of nowhere and I was running on empty; fortunately, a gas station was up ahead. As I pulled in, the man looked like he had not had a customer all week. He got up with a big smile on his face and wanted to fill my tank—assistance which for a motorcycle is unusual, even at "full-service" stations. But he insisted and talked up a storm like he was my old buddy. As the pump ticked, one observation after another came out of his mouth: on the weather, something about the Texas governor, even something about his kid's bicycle, until he noticed my license plate. He looked at it like he had never seen one before; just stopped in his tracks.

"California!" Suspicion was now on his face. In his strong Southern drawl, he remarked, "I heard there was a lot of homo sex-u-als in California." I thought this over to myself. I am decidedly heterosexual, and wondered what his problem was. "Maybe you're thinking of San Francisco," I countered. "Anyway, they never bothered me."

He continued staring, unimpressed by my reply. I love the rural South, but was really provoked by the continuing condescending gleam in his eye. He kept staring at me like I was an animal in a zoo, and I felt a need to come back at him with some comment of my own: "I heard there were a lot of racists in these parts." There was another long pause. His Texas-sized belly wiggled through his shirt as he walked around me slowly.

Finally, his expression relaxed, his smile returned, and he concluded this round with, "Well... it takes allllll kinds."

EPILOGUE

⌃
‹ I take a stroll on the Bering Sea near Kotzebue, Alaska.

You may be wondering how in the world this guy can afford to do so much traveling. The answer is by going low budget. In developing countries, a good meal need not cost more than a dollar and accommodations are often under $10. Even in expensive Europe or Japan, youth hostels and rail passes can help keep expenses in check. Instead of high-priced flights, a second- or third-class train ticket, a cheap local bus, a motorbike, or a lift on the back of a donkey cart can usually prove the old adage that getting there is half the fun. A costly necessity may be flying across the pond—that is, the Atlantic or Pacific Ocean—but even those costs can be minimized with a little effort and flexibility. I have gotten as far as LAX to Singapore on a $200 courier flight.

Most people have either the time or the money to travel, but not both. Time is far more important than money, and attitude more important than anything. Take only a small backpack (limiting your luggage is important). Travel mode and manner are key; spontaneity is essential. Traveling alone will make all kinds of invitations more likely. And in most places, expecting American-style hotels or food and other amenities would be as strange as a Japanese person requiring a traditional Japanese bed and bath on a trip to the U.S.A. Many people do travel that way, but they are limiting themselves to fancy districts in only a few cities. And worse, they are insulating themselves from many enjoyable aspects of the country, not to mention running up an exorbitant price tag.

Some take tours or go to a resort. Unfortunately, tours also can insulate you from the best things a place has to offer, especially the local people. It is not likely that on a tour you would be invited to someone's home or have much other intimate contact with a culture. With limited time off for many Americans, it may be a choice between a tour or no trip at all. Short vacations, in my opinion, may very well be America's worst problem.

Most people have little experience outside their country and suffer for it. I'd like to quote Mark Twain again: "Travel is fatal to prejudice, bigotry and narrow-mindedness, and many of our people need it sorely on these accounts. Broad, wholesome, charitable views of men and things can not be acquired by vegetating in one little corner of the earth all one's lifetime."

Travel can be more educational than a classroom at any school; it can be more fulfilling than time spent doing many other things. Travel can offer remarkable rewards. But aren't going to some of those remote places dangerous? Is it worth the risk? The news has us believe that the world is full of terrible things, war and turmoil, things surely not welcoming to a vulnerable independent traveler. There is no doubt you must be careful in some places.

Reality, for me though, is clear. With extensive experience all over the planet, the most dangerous place I have been is down a few blocks from my house, here in Los Angeles.

All photographs, besides the three postcards on page 233, were either taken by my Pentex IQ Zoom or my favorite old Pentex ME Super. The latter, unfortunately, fell into a swamp.

Teaching my daughters to ski began at an early age.

The
End